Mastering Multiplication Tables

Fun games and activities to play with your child

By Chris James

Version 1.0

Published on November 20th 2013

Contents

Introduction

Learning Your Times Tables

Love them or loath them, the multiplication tables are one of the mathematical basics that your child simply has to learn. They are important to know in their own right but they will also underpin large sections of their number work as they grow older, and will open the door to working with larger numbers.

The times tables are not though easy to learn and this book attempts to take some of the pain out of the process. It covers all of the tables, up to and including the 12 Times Table. This may in fact be beyond what your child is expected to learn at school, depending on which curriculum they follow. Some countries, for example, only require children to learn up to the 10 times table. I do though find that the 11 and 12 times tables are extremely useful to know. I have therefore written the book, assuming that you wish your child to learn up to this level.

There are 3 main chapters to this book. The first chapter explains how you can teach the times tables to your child, through a combination of visual and kinesthetic experiences.

Having done this, there is a chapter detailing 10 games for you, a sibling or a friend to play with your child; to help them to remember the times tables that they have been working on. Some of the games require little or no preparation, while others require you to photocopy the resources that are included in the book.

The final step to learning the times tables is for your child to able to recall them in a test type situation. The last chapter of the book therefore consists of a series of practice questions.

When Should You Start Teaching Your Child?

I would recommend that you first start teaching the times tables to your child when they are about six or seven years old, and that they should confidently know them all by the time that they are nine. This is of course only a guide and you need to be aware that different children have different abilities and progress at different rates. Some children will therefore be ready to learn their times tables earlier than the age of six, while others will have to wait until they are older than seven. You will only get to know what your child is capable of by working with them and trying some of the activities in this book. It is though important that you do not try to force your child before they are ready. There is no point trying to cram information into them at an early age, when they do not understand what they are doing. This is likely to lead to confusion later on and may in fact be detrimental to their learning.

Also, try not to get frustrated with your child if they are not learning at the rate that you hope for. They won't be purposely trying to make mistakes. It is just that they find it hard. Your child will always learn more effectively in a happy, supportive environment. Therefore try to encourage your child and offer as much positive praise as possible. It is though important that you are specific in the praise that you use. For example; rather than just saying a general "Well done!" try to highlight exactly what they have done well by saying something like, "Well done for remembering that 6 x 7 is 42," or "Excellent; you recalled those tables much quicker than yesterday."

In What Order Should Your Child Learn The Times Tables?

Before I go on to giving you advice on how to teach the tables, it should be pointed out that the order that your child learns the times tables should not necessarily be in straight sequential order. I have written below the sequence that I normally teach the times tables in the classroom, but this may not be the order that your child is asked to learn them at school. I therefore recommend that you speak to your child's teacher and adjust the order to fit it in with what they are learning in the classroom.

My Recommended Order

• The one times table, because the pattern is simple.
• The ten times table, because of its link to the one times table.
• The eleven times table, because it is a combination of the ten and one times table.
• The five times table, because half of the answers are also in the ten times table.
• The two times table, because doubling is an important skill.
• The four times table, because it is the double of the two times table.
• The eight times table, because it is the double of the four times table.
• The three times table, because it helps to learn it before the six and twelve times tables.
• The six times table, because it is the double of the three times table.
• The twelve times table, because it is the double of the six times table.
• The nine times table, because it has some interesting patterns.
• The seven times table, because this is normally the hardest times table to learn.

Spotting Patterns

Spotting patterns is a very important mathematical skill. When your child is learning a times table it is therefore important that you explore the patterns in the answers. You should firstly ask your child if they can see any patterns for themselves, rather than just spoon feeding them the answer. If they struggle to recognise any patterns, try to lead them into the answer. For example, if you are looking at the 5 times tables you could ask your child, "What do you notice about the last digit in the answers?" They will hopefully then be able to spot that all of the answers end in either a 5 or a 0. If after some gentle coaxing they still cannot see the pattern, then it's time for you to step in. Don't though be tempted to jump in too quickly. Always give your child plenty of time to think. The following are the main patterns, although your child might discover something completely different:

The Main Patterns

• The one times table: the answers are the same as the first line of the times table for example **4 x 1 = 4**

• The two times table: all of the answers are even.

• The three times table: there is no really helpful pattern apart from the fact that the answers alternate from even to odd all through the times table.

• The four times table: again, because four is an even number, all of the answers are even.

• The five times table: the answers alternate between ending in five and zero.

• The six times table: again, because six is an even number, all of the answers are even.

• The seven times table: there is no really helpful pattern apart from the fact that the answers alternate from odd to even all through the times table.

• The eight times table: again, because eight is an even number, all of the answers are even.

• The nine times table: when you add up the digits in the answer, it always gives you the answer nine. For example; 9 x 9 = 81 and 8 + 1 equals nine. With 11 x 9 = 99 you have to add the digits twice i.e. 9 + 9 = 18 and then 1 + 8 = 9.

• The ten times table: the answer always ends in zero.

For future reference; children are often taught that when you multiply by ten, you simply add a zero. While this is, strictly speaking, true for whole numbers (called integers) it does not hold true when multiplying decimals. If you multiply 0.9 by 10 for example it does not equal 0.90 but 9. This is because the number moves one place to the left. Try therefore to avoid telling your child that a zero is added to the number so that they don't have to unlearn this at a later date.

• The eleven times table: for the first nine sums in the eleven times table, both of the digits are the same.

• The twelve times table: once again, as twelve is an even number, all of the answers are even.

Right, now it's time to actually start teaching the tables to your child.........

Chapter 1: How To Teach The Times Tables

Phase 1: Making

This first phase requires your child to build a physical model of each sum in the times table that you want to work on. This is known as kinesthetic learning. By making a concrete example your child will get to understand the process behind each of the times tables and therefore retain the information more readily. This can be done with any sets of objects, such as Lego or sweets, or can be done using a set of mathematical cubes. It is basically best to use anything that your child finds appealing. I have chosen to show them in the following examples using commercially available cubes. To begin with, each sum in the times tables should be thought of as a group of objects.

For example; 1 x 4 is one group of four, which equals four. This will be shown as one group of four cubes.

2 x 4 is two groups of four, which equals eight. This should be shown as two groups of four cubes.

Each time that a sum is made it is essential that your child also says the sum out loud. For example, when one group of four cubes is made, you should ask something like, "What have you made?" You should encourage them to reply with, "One group of four makes four." And when they make two groups of four, they should say, "Two groups of four make eight."

This process should be repeated until 12 groups of the cubes have been made. It's important though to build these up in order. However, your child does not necessarily have to learn all of the facts for a times table at once. In one session they should learn as much of the times tables as their concentration span allows. As a general rule of thumb, a child can concentrate for 5 minutes plus their age. An average six year old child should therefore be able to concentrate for 5 + 6 = 11 minutes at a time. Some children will be able to concentrate for longer than this and some will only be able to concentrate for a shorter period of time. It is though counterproductive to try to do too much at once, especially if you are trying to work with your child after a busy day at school. I have young children of my own and I find that three short sessions of 10 minutes each, spaced over the course of a week, are more effective than one session of 30 minutes. You though know your child better than anyone, so you should be able to judge what they can and cannot achieve. Don't though be tempted to overdo things, as you may end up putting them off altogether.

The next step is to represent each multiplication sum in rows and columns. This is referred to as an array. It has the advantage over just grouping the objects in that it shows that 6 x 4 is the same as 4 x 6. This is an important concept that children have to learn and should be discussed as the children build their arrays. Each array should look something like this:

Again, ask your child to verbalize what they have made. You should be looking for a reply which is something like, "Four rows of six make twenty four," or "Six lots of four make twenty four."

When your child has become confident building groups and arrays for the times table that you are working on, it is time to move on to phase 2.

Phase 2: Coloring

During the next phase your child should represent each of the arrays that they made during phase 1, by coloring in the correct number of squares on a piece of squared paper. Creating these visual prompts will help to reinforce each of the number facts in turn and make it easier for them to remember them over time. Again, it is important that your child verbalizes what they are doing, so that when they have colored in three groups of four to make twelve they need to say, "Three groups of four make twelve."

I have included an example below of what these drawings should look like:

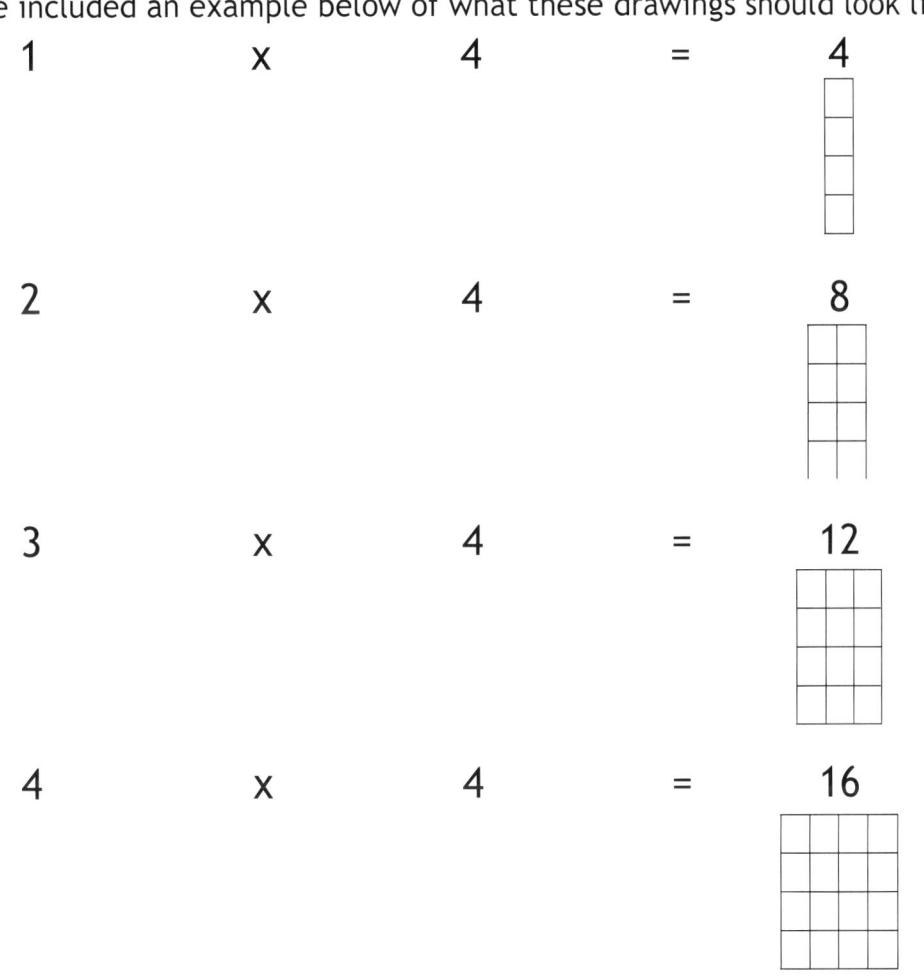

Once your child has completed both the making and coloring stages it is time to play some of the times tables games.

Chapter 2: Times Tables Games

All of the following games are ones that I currently use with my class. I know that the children find them fun and engaging and they definitely help their learning. Some of the games require the resources that come with the book, while others require no preparation at all.

Activity 1: Multiplication Dice

A game for 2 or more players
Equipment: 2 Dice, a Pencil, Paper and the Multiplication Grid
Player one rolls the 2 dice. They must then multiply the score from one dice with the score from the other dice to get an answer. For example, 6 x 5 = 30

Player two should then check this answer using the multiplication grid. If the answer is correct, player one writes down their score on a piece of paper. If they give an incorrect answer, they score zero. It is then player two's turn to roll the dice and make a multiplication sum. Play continues in this way, but each time that a player correctly answers a question they should add their score to their previous total. The first player to reach 301 is the winner. This target amount can though be changed, up or down, depending on the ability of your child.

Conventional dice do though only have the digits 1 to 6 and can therefore only test up to six times six. However, it is possible to buy mathematical dice which have the numbers 1 to 12. Alternatively, both dice can be rolled and their total can be used to create the first number in the multiplication sum. Depending on what times tables you want to work on, the second number in the question can then either be generated using a single dice (to test the tables from 1 to 6) or both dice (to test the tables from 1 to 12). If you want to make the times table that you are testing even more specific, you can put small sticky labels over the faces on the dice and write in the numbers that you want. If, for example, you are just working on the 1, 2, 4, 5, 10 and 11 times tables you need to make stickers with 10 and 11 on them to cover up the faces on a dice with 3 and 6 on them.

Multiplication Grid

x	1	2	3	4	5	6	7	8	9	10	11	12
1	1	2	3	4	5	6	7	8	9	10	11	12
2	2	4	6	8	10	12	14	16	18	20	22	24
3	3	6	9	12	15	18	21	24	27	30	33	36
4	4	8	12	16	20	24	28	32	36	40	44	48
5	5	10	15	20	25	30	35	40	45	50	55	60
6	6	12	18	24	30	36	42	48	54	60	66	72
7	7	14	21	28	35	42	49	56	63	70	77	84
8	8	16	24	32	40	48	56	64	72	80	88	96
9	9	18	27	36	45	54	63	72	81	90	99	108
10	10	20	30	40	50	60	70	80	90	100	110	120
11	11	22	33	44	55	66	77	88	99	110	121	132
12	12	24	36	48	60	72	84	96	108	120	132	144

Activity 2: Buzz

A game for two or more players

Equipment: The Multiplication Grid

To play Buzz you must choose a times table that you want to practice. The players then take it in turns to count from one upwards. When they reach a number that is in that times table they say *Buzz* rather than the number. For example if you are playing with Buzz as five, you would start off 1, 2, 3, 4, *Buzz*, 6, 7, 8, 9, *Buzz*. Play continues until you reach the multiple of 12, in this case 12 x 5 = 60.

All players start with 10 points. If a child makes a mistake, by saying *Buzz* at the wrong time or not saying *Buzz* at the right time, they lose a point. The winner is the child with the most number of points at the end of the game.

The game can be extended to Fizz, Buzz where *Fizz* is said instead of the multiples of one number and *Buzz* is said instead of the multiples of another number. If a number in the sequence is a multiple of just one of the numbers, you need to say *Fizz* or *Buzz*, but if the number is a multiple of both numbers, you need to say *Fizz, Buzz*.

If necessary, the answers can be checked using the multiplication grid.

Activity 3: Matching Pairs Game

A game for 2 or more players

Equipment: Matching Pairs Cards and the Multiplication Grid

In this section there is a set of matching pairs cards for each of the multiplication tables. For each multiplication table there are 12 question cards and 12 answer cards. These need to be photocopied, cut out and spread face down on a table; with the question cards in a different group from the answer cards. Player one then turns over a question card, followed by an answer card. If the question card and the answer card match up, they keep that pair of cards. They then have a go at trying to find another pair of matching cards. They continue until the pair of cards that they turn over does not match. Player two then has their turn. When their turn is finished, player one has another go and the game continues until all the cards have been matched up. The winner is the player with the most number of cards at the end of the game. Any disputes over whether a pair of cards matches or not should be settled using the Multiplication Grid.

Matching Pairs Game Cards

# 12 x 1 Pairs Game: 1 Times Table	# = 12 Pairs Game: 1 Times Table
# 11 x 1 Pairs Game: 1 Times Table	# = 11 Pairs Game: 1 Times Table
# 10 x 1 Pairs Game: 1 Times Table	# = 10 Pairs Game: 1 Times Table
# 9 x 1 Pairs Game: 1 Times Table	# = 9 Pairs Game: 1 Times Table
# 8 x 1 Pairs Game: 1 Times Table	# = 8 Pairs Game: 1 Times Table
# 7 x 1 Pairs Game: 1 Times Table	# = 7 Pairs Game: 1 Times Table
# 6 x 1 Pairs Game: 1 Times Table	# = 6 Pairs Game: 1 Times Table

5 x 1	**=** **5**
Pairs Game: 1 Times Table	Pairs Game: 1 Times Table
4 x 1	**=** **4**
Pairs Game: 1 Times Table	Pairs Game: 1 Times Table
3 x 1	**=** **3**
Pairs Game: 1 Times Table	Pairs Game: 1 Times Table
2 x 1	**=** **2**
Pairs Game: 1 Times Table	Pairs Game: 1 Times Table
1 x 1	**=** **1**
Pairs Game: 1 Times Table	Pairs Game: 1 Times Table
12 x 2	**=** **24**
Pairs Game: 2 Times Table	Pairs Game: 2 Times Table
11 x 2	**=** **22**
Pairs Game: 2 Times Table	Pairs Game: 2 Times Table

# 10 x 2 Pairs Game: 2 Times Table	# = 20 Pairs Game: 2 Times Table
# 9 x 2 Pairs Game: 2 Times Table	# = 18 Pairs Game: 2 Times Table
# 8 x 2 Pairs Game: 2 Times Table	# = 16 Pairs Game: 2 Times Table
# 7 x 2 Pairs Game: 2 Times Table	# = 14 Pairs Game: 2 Times Table
# 6 x 2 Pairs Game: 2 Times Table	# = 12 Pairs Game: 2 Times Table
# 5 x 2 Pairs Game: 2 Times Table	# = 10 Pairs Game: 2 Times Table
# 4 x 2 Pairs Game: 2 Times Table	# = 8 Pairs Game: 2 Times Table

3×2	$= 6$
Pairs Game: 2 Times Table	Pairs Game: 2 Times Table
2×2	$= 4$
Pairs Game: 2 Times Table	Pairs Game: 2 Times Table
1×2	$= 2$
Pairs Game: 2 Times Table	Pairs Game: 2 Times Table
12×3	$= 36$
Pairs Game: 3 Times Table	Pairs Game: 3 Times Table
11×3	$= 33$
Pairs Game: 3 Times Table	Pairs Game: 3 Times Table
10×3	$= 30$
Pairs Game: 3 Times Table	Pairs Game: 3 Times Table
9×3	$= 27$
Pairs Game: 3 Times Table	Pairs Game: 3 Times Table

8 x 3	= 24
Pairs Game: 3 Times Table	Pairs Game: 3 Times Table
7 x 3	= 21
Pairs Game: 3 Times Table	Pairs Game: 3 Times Table
6 x 3	= 18
Pairs Game: 3 Times Table	Pairs Game: 3 Times Table
5 x 3	= 15
Pairs Game: 3 Times Table	Pairs Game: 3 Times Table
4 x 3	= 12
Pairs Game: 3 Times Table	Pairs Game: 3 Times Table
3 x 3	= 9
Pairs Game: 3 Times Table	Pairs Game: 3 Times Table
2 x 3	= 6
Pairs Game: 3 Times Table	Pairs Game: 3 Times Table

1 x 3	= 3
Pairs Game: 4 Times Table	Pairs Game: 3 Times Table
12 x 4	= 48
Pairs Game: 4 Times Table	Pairs Game: 4 Times Table
11 x 4	= 44
Pairs Game: 4 Times Table	Pairs Game: 4 Times Table
10 x 4	= 40
Pairs Game: 4 Times Table	Pairs Game: 4 Times Table
9 x 4	= 36
Pairs Game: 4 Times Table	Pairs Game: 4 Times Table
8 x 4	= 32
Pairs Game: 4 Times Table	Pairs Game: 4 Times Table
7 x 4	= 28
Pairs Game: 4 Times Table	Pairs Game: 4 Times Table

6 x 4	= 24
Pairs Game: 4 Times Table	Pairs Game: 4 Times Table
5 x 4	= 20
Pairs Game: 4 Times Table	Pairs Game: 4 Times Table
4 x 4	= 16
Pairs Game: 4 Times Table	Pairs Game: 4 Times Table
3 x 4	= 12
Pairs Game: 4 Times Table	Pairs Game: 4 Times Table
2 x 4	= 8
Pairs Game: 4 Times Table	Pairs Game: 4 Times Table
1 x 4	= 4
Pairs Game: 4 Times Table	Pairs Game: 4 Times Table
12 x 5	= 60
Pairs Game: 5 Times Table	Pairs Game: 5 Times Table

# 11 x 5 Pairs Game: 5 Times Table	# = 55 Pairs Game: 5 Times Table
# 10 x 5 Pairs Game: 5 Times Table	# = 50 Pairs Game: 5 Times Table
# 9 x 5 Pairs Game: 5 Times Table	# = 45 Pairs Game: 5 Times Table
# 8 x 5 Pairs Game: 5 Times Table	# = 40 Pairs Game: 5 Times Table
# 7 x 5 Pairs Game: 5 Times Table	# = 35 Pairs Game: 5 Times Table
# 6 x 5 Pairs Game: 5 Times Table	# = 30 Pairs Game: 5 Times Table
# 5 x 5 Pairs Game: 5 Times Table	# = 25 Pairs Game: 5 Times Table

# 4 x 5 Pairs Game: 5 Times Table	# = 20 Pairs Game: 5 Times Table
# 3 x 5 Pairs Game: 5 Times Table	# = 15 Pairs Game: 5 Times Table
# 2 x 5 Pairs Game: 5 Times Table	# = 10 Pairs Game: 5 Times Table
# 1 x 5 Pairs Game: 5 Times Table	# = 5 Pairs Game: 5 Times Table
# 12 x 6 Pairs Game: 6 Times Table	# = 72 Pairs Game: 6 Times Table
# 11 x 6 Pairs Game: 6 Times Table	# = 66 Pairs Game: 6 Times Table
# 10 x 6 Pairs Game: 6 Times Table	# = 60 Pairs Game: 6 Times Table

9 x 6	= 54
Pairs Game: 6 Times Table	Pairs Game: 6 Times Table
8 x 6	= 48
Pairs Game: 6 Times Table	Pairs Game: 6 Times Table
7 x 6	= 42
Pairs Game: 6 Times Table	Pairs Game: 6 Times Table
6 x 6	= 36
Pairs Game: 6 Times Table	Pairs Game: 6 Times Table
5 x 6	= 30
Pairs Game: 6 Times Table	Pairs Game: 6 Times Table
4 x 6	= 24
Pairs Game: 6 Times Table	Pairs Game: 6 Times Table
3 x 6	= 18
Pairs Game: 6 Times Table	Pairs Game: 6 Times Table

2 x 6	= 12
Pairs Game: 6 Times Table	Pairs Game: 6 Times Table
1 x 6	= 6
Pairs Game: 6 Times Table	Pairs Game: 6 Times Table
12 x 7	= 84
Pairs Game: 7 Times Table	Pairs Game: 7 Times Table
11 x 7	= 77
Pairs Game: 7 Times Table	Pairs Game: 7 Times Table
10 x 7	= 70
Pairs Game: 7 Times Table	Pairs Game: 7 Times Table
9 x 7	= 63
Pairs Game: 7 Times Table	Pairs Game: 7 Times Table
8 x 7	= 56
Pairs Game: 7 Times Table	Pairs Game: 7 Times Table

# 7 x 7	# = 49
Pairs Game: 7 Times Table	Pairs Game: 7 Times Table
# 6 x 7	# = 42
Pairs Game: 7 Times Table	Pairs Game: 7 Times Table
# 5 x 7	# = 35
Pairs Game: 7 Times Table	Pairs Game: 7 Times Table
# 4 x 7	# = 28
Pairs Game: 7 Times Table	Pairs Game: 7 Times Table
# 3 x 7	# = 21
Pairs Game: 7 Times Table	Pairs Game: 7 Times Table
# 2 x 7	# = 14
Pairs Game: 7 Times Table	Pairs Game: 7 Times Table
# 1 x 7	# = 7
Pairs Game: 7 Times Table	Pairs Game: 7 Times Table

12 x 8	= 96
Pairs Game: 8 Times Table	Pairs Game: 8 Times Table
11 x 8	= 88
Pairs Game: 8 Times Table	Pairs Game: 8 Times Table
10 x 8	= 80
Pairs Game: 8 Times Table	Pairs Game: 8 Times Table
9 x 8	= 72
Pairs Game: 8 Times Table	Pairs Game: 8 Times Table
8 x 8	= 64
Pairs Game: 8 Times Table	Pairs Game: 8 Times Table
7 x 8	= 56
Pairs Game: 8 Times Table	Pairs Game: 8 Times Table
6 x 8	= 48
Pairs Game: 8 Times Table	Pairs Game: 8 Times Table

5 x 8	= 40
Pairs Game: 8 Times Table	Pairs Game: 8 Times Table
4 x 8	= 32
Pairs Game: 8 Times Table	Pairs Game: 8 Times Table
3 x 8	= 24
Pairs Game: 8 Times Table	Pairs Game: 8 Times Table
2 x 8	= 16
Pairs Game: 8 Times Table	Pairs Game: 8 Times Table
1 x 8	= 8
Pairs Game: 8 Times Table	Pairs Game: 8 Times Table
12 x 9	= 108
Pairs Game: 9 Times Table	Pairs Game: 9 Times Table
11 x 9	= 99
Pairs Game: 9 Times Table	Pairs Game: 9 Times Table

10×9	$= 90$
Pairs Game: 9 Times Table	*Pairs Game: 9 Times Table*
9×9	$= 81$
Pairs Game: 9 Times Table	*Pairs Game: 9 Times Table*
8×9	$= 72$
Pairs Game: 9 Times Table	*Pairs Game: 9 Times Table*
7×9	$= 63$
Pairs Game: 9 Times Table	*Pairs Game: 9 Times Table*
6×9	$= 54$
Pairs Game: 9 Times Table	*Pairs Game: 9 Times Table*
5×9	$= 45$
Pairs Game: 9 Times Table	*Pairs Game: 9 Times Table*
4×9	$= 36$
Pairs Game: 9 Times Table	*Pairs Game: 9 Times Table*

3 x 9	= 27
Pairs Game: 9 Times Table	Pairs Game: 9 Times Table
2 x 9	= 18
Pairs Game: 9 Times Table	Pairs Game: 9 Times Table
1 x 9	= 9
Pairs Game: 9 Times Table	Pairs Game: 9 Times Table
12 x 10	= 120
Pairs Game: 10 Times Table	Pairs Game: 10 Times Table
11 x 10	= 110
Pairs Game: 10 Times Table	Pairs Game: 10 Times Table
10 x 10	= 100
Pairs Game: 10 Times Table	Pairs Game: 10 Times Table
9 x 10	= 90
Pairs Game: 10 Times Table	Pairs Game: 10 Times Table

8 x 10	= 80
Pairs Game: 10 Times Table	Pairs Game: 10 Times Table
7 x 10	= 70
Pairs Game: 10 Times Table	Pairs Game: 10 Times Table
6 x 10	= 60
Pairs Game: 10 Times Table	Pairs Game: 10 Times Table
5 x 10	= 50
Pairs Game: 10 Times Table	Pairs Game: 10 Times Table
4 x 10	= 40
Pairs Game: 10 Times Table	Pairs Game: 10 Times Table
3 x 10	= 30
Pairs Game: 10 Times Table	Pairs Game: 10 Times Table
2 x 10	= 20
Pairs Game: 10 Times Table	Pairs Game: 10 Times Table

# 1 x 10	# = 10
Pairs Game: 10 Times Table	Pairs Game: 10 Times Table
# 12 x 11	# = 132
Pairs Game: 11 Times Table	Pairs Game: 11 Times Table
# 11 x 11	# = 121
Pairs Game: 11 Times Table	Pairs Game: 11 Times Table
# 10 x 11	# = 110
Pairs Game: 11 Times Table	Pairs Game: 11 Times Table
# 9 x 11	# = 99
Pairs Game: 11 Times Table	Pairs Game: 11 Times Table
# 8 x 11	# = 88
Pairs Game: 11 Times Table	Pairs Game: 11 Times Table
# 7 x 11	# = 77
Pairs Game: 11 Times Table	Pairs Game: 11 Times Table

# 6 x 11 Pairs Game: 11 Times Table	# = 66 Pairs Game: 11 Times Table
# 5 x 11 Pairs Game: 11 Times Table	# = 55 Pairs Game: 11 Times Table
# 4 x 11 Pairs Game: 11 Times Table	# = 44 Pairs Game: 11 Times Table
# 3 x 11 Pairs Game: 11 Times Table	# = 33 Pairs Game: 11 Times Table
# 2 x 11 Pairs Game: 11 Times Table	# = 22 Pairs Game: 11 Times Table
# 1 x 11 Pairs Game: 11 Times Table	# = 11 Pairs Game: 11 Times Table
# 12 x 12 Pairs Game: 12 Times Table	# = 144 Pairs Game: 12 Times Table

11 x 12	= 132
Pairs Game: 12 Times Table	Pairs Game: 12 Times Table
10 x 12	= 120
Pairs Game: 12 Times Table	Pairs Game: 12 Times Table
9 x 12	= 108
Pairs Game: 12 Times Table	Pairs Game: 12 Times Table
8 x 12	= 96
Pairs Game: 12 Times Table	Pairs Game: 12 Times Table
7 x 12	= 84
Pairs Game: 12 Times Table	Pairs Game: 12 Times Table
6 x 12	= 72
Pairs Game: 12 Times Table	Pairs Game: 12 Times Table
5 x 12	= 60
Pairs Game: 12 Times Table	Pairs Game: 12 Times Table

4 x 12	= 48
Pairs Game: 12 Times Table	Pairs Game: 12 Times Table
3 x 12	= 36
Pairs Game: 12 Times Table	Pairs Game: 12 Times Table
2 x 12	= 24
Pairs Game: 12 Times Table	Pairs Game: 12 Times Table
1 x 12	= 12
Pairs Game: 12 Times Table	Pairs Game: 12 Times Table

Activity 4: Multiplication Dice Game Two

A game for two or more players

Equipment: The *Answer* Cards from the Matching Pairs Game, 2 Dice and the Multiplication Grid

You firstly need to decide on the times table that you want to practise. Then select the appropriate *answer* cards only from the Matching Pairs Game. These should be placed face up on the table, so that all of the answers can be seen. The lowest value answer card (the one which answers the question 1 x ?) should be removed and put to one side. Player one then rolls the two dice and adds the scores together. He or she can then pick up the card which links to that number in the multiplication table that they are using. For example, if you are playing with the seven times table and somebody rolls a two and a three which makes **five**, they are able to then pick up the card which has 35 on because **5** x 7 =35. Play then passes on to the next person. If a player rolls a total for a card that has already been taken, they cannot pick up a card and play passes onto next player. When all of the cards have been used up, each player counts their cards and the player with the most number of cards is the winner. If necessary, the answers can be checked using the multiplication grid.

Activity 5: Multiplication Bingo

A game for between 2 and 4 players

Equipment: Bingo Cards, Question Cards, Counters and the Multiplication Grid

Firstly, photocopy and cut out the 4 bingo cards and the set of 60 question cards that are included in this section.

Each player needs a bingo card, and the question cards are placed face down in the middle of the table. Play starts when one of the players turns over a question card. Each player tries to work out the answer in their heads. If they have the answer on their bingo card they should call out the answer. The answer can then be checked using the multiplication grid. If the answer is correct, the child can then cover the corresponding square on their bingo card with one of the counters provided. The question card is then put to one side.

If a child calls out an answer which when checked is found to be incorrect, the card is put back to the bottom of the pile. It is possible that another player might at this point discover that they in fact have the answer on their card. They cannot though now claim it, as it has already been checked on the multiplication square, and they must wait until the card comes up again.

If nobody claims a card, it should be put back to the bottom of the pile.

Play continues in this fashion until one of the players has covered all of the squares on their bingo card. They are the winner.

The question cards for this game cover questions from all of the times tables. Your child therefore needs to have learnt all of the times tables before they play Multiplication Bingo.

In order to create 4 bingo cards I had to duplicate some of the numbers. The numbers 32, 54, 60, 63, 66 and 72 each appear on two different cards. There are therefore two different question cards that give these numbers as the answer. If two players call for the same number, it is the player that calls first that gets to cover their square.

Bingo Cards

144	32	15	49
63	48	44	8
12	80	110	64
55	72	20	22

96	70	42	35
108	72	21	132
27	3	81	60
11	28	4	90

6	63	5	16
88	50	30	100
54	10	45	60
84	25	99	66

9	54	77	36
120	2	14	56
24	66	121	40
33	18	7	32

Bingo Question Cards

# 12 x 12 Bingo	# 11 x 12 Bingo
# 12 x 10 Bingo	# 9 x 12 Bingo
# 12 x 8 Bingo	# 7 x 12 Bingo
# 1 x 1 Bingo	# 5 x 12 Bingo
# 6 x 8 Bingo	# 6 x 6 Bingo
# 8 x 3 Bingo	# 3 x 4 Bingo
# 11 x 11 Bingo	# 10 x 11 Bingo

11 x 9	8 x 11
Bingo	Bingo
11 x 7	6 x 11
Bingo	Bingo
11 x 5	4 x 11
Bingo	Bingo
11 x 3	2 x 11
Bingo	Bingo
1 x 11	10 x 10
Bingo	Bingo
10 x 9	8 x 10
Bingo	Bingo
10 x 7	5 x 10
Bingo	Bingo

5 x 8 Bingo	5 x 6 Bingo
5 x 4 Bingo	2 x 5 Bingo
9 x 9 Bingo	8 x 9 Bingo
9 x 7 Bingo	6 x 9 Bingo
5 x 9 Bingo	9 x 3 Bingo
2 x 9 Bingo	3 x 3 Bingo
8 x 8 Bingo	8 x 7 Bingo

4 x 8	2 x 8
Bingo	Bingo
4 x 2	7 x 7
Bingo	Bingo
7 x 6	5 x 7
Bingo	Bingo
7 x 4	3 x 7
Bingo	Bingo
7 x 2	1 x 7
Bingo	Bingo
2 x 3	5 x 5
Bingo	Bingo
3 x 5	5 x 1
Bingo	Bingo

2 x 2 Bingo	1 x 3 Bingo
2 x 1 Bingo	12 x 6 Bingo
8 x 4 Bingo	9 x 6 Bingo
12 x 5 Bingo	7 x 9 Bingo
11 x 6 Bingo	

Bingo Counters

Bingo Counter	Bingo Counter	Bingo Counter	Bingo Counter
Bingo Counter	Bingo Counter	Bingo Counter	Bingo Counter
Bingo Counter	Bingo Counter	Bingo Counter	Bingo Counter
Bingo Counter	Bingo Counter	Bingo Counter	Bingo Counter

Bingo Counter	Bingo Counter	Bingo Counter	Bingo Counter
Bingo Counter	Bingo Counter	Bingo Counter	Bingo Counter
Bingo Counter	Bingo Counter	Bingo Counter	Bingo Counter
Bingo Counter	Bingo Counter	Bingo Counter	Bingo Counter

Bingo Counter	Bingo Counter	Bingo Counter	Bingo Counter
Bingo Counter	Bingo Counter	Bingo Counter	Bingo Counter
Bingo Counter	Bingo Counter	Bingo Counter	Bingo Counter
Bingo Counter	Bingo Counter	Bingo Counter	Bingo Counter

Bingo Counter	Bingo Counter	Bingo Counter	Bingo Counter
Bingo Counter	Bingo Counter	Bingo Counter	Bingo Counter
Bingo Counter	Bingo Counter	Bingo Counter	Bingo Counter
Bingo Counter	Bingo Counter	Bingo Counter	Bingo Counter

Activity 6: Quick Fire Tables

A game for 3 to 4 players

Equipment: Quick Fire Tables Cards

Firstly, photocopy and cut out the cards for one of the sets of Quick Fire Cards from the following pages.

Each of the sets has 12 question cards. To start the game, player one turns over a question card and reads it out. The first player, who cannot be the caller, who calls out the correct answer keeps the card. The answer is given on the bottom right-hand side of the card should the caller need to check. The cards are then passed clockwise to the next player. He or she repeats the process. When all of the cards have been claimed the players count their cards. The player with the most number of cards is the winner.

A longer, more complicated version of the game can be played by mixing two or more of the packs together.

Quick Fire Tables Cards

# 12 x 1 Quick Fire: 1 Times Table — Answer = 12	# 6 x 1 Quick Fire: 1 Times Table — Answer = 6
# 11 x 1 Quick Fire: 1 Times Table — Answer = 11	# 5 x 1 Quick Fire: 1 Times Table — Answer = 5
# 10 x 1 Quick Fire: 1 Times Table — Answer = 10	# 4 x 1 Quick Fire: 1 Times Table — Answer = 4
# 9 x 1 Quick Fire: 1 Times Table — Answer = 9	# 3 x 1 Quick Fire: 1 Times Table — Answer = 3
# 8 x 1 Quick Fire: 1 Times Table — Answer = 8	# 2 x 1 Quick Fire: 1 Times Table — Answer = 2
# 7 x 1 Quick Fire: 1 Times Table — Answer = 7	# 1 x 1 Quick Fire: 1 Times Table — Answer = 1
# 12 x 2 Quick Fire: 2 Times Table — Answer = 24	# 6 x 2 Quick Fire: 2 Times Table — Answer = 12

11 x 2	5 x 2
Quick Fire: 2 Times Table Answer = 22	Quick Fire: 2 Times Table Answer = 10
10 x 2	4 x 2
Quick Fire: 2 Times Table Answer = 20	Quick Fire: 2 Times Table Answer = 8
9 x 2	3 x 2
Quick Fire: 2 Times Table Answer = 18	Quick Fire: 2 Times Table Answer = 6
8 x 2	2 x 2
Quick Fire: 2 Times Table Answer = 16	Quick Fire: 2 Times Table Answer = 4
7 x 2	1 x 2
Quick Fire: 2 Times Table Answer = 14	Quick Fire: 2 Times Table Answer = 2
12 x 3	6 x 3
Quick Fire: 3 Times Table Answer = 36	Quick Fire: 3 Times Table Answer = 18
11 x 3	5 x 3
Quick Fire: 3 Times Table Answer = 33	Quick Fire: 3 Times Table Answer = 15

10 x 3 Quick Fire: 3 Times Table Answer = 27	**4 x 3** Quick Fire: 3 Times Table Answer = 9
9 x 3 Quick Fire: 3 Times Table Answer = 27	**3 x 3** Quick Fire: 3 Times Table Answer = 9
8 x 3 Quick Fire: 3 Times Table Answer = 24	**2 x 3** Quick Fire: 3 Times Table Answer = 6
7 x 3 Quick Fire: 3 Times Table Answer = 21	**1 x 3** Quick Fire: 3 Times Table Answer = 3
12 x 4 Quick Fire: 4 Times Table Answer = 48	**6 x 4** Quick Fire: 4 Times Table Answer = 24
11 x 4 Quick Fire: 4 Times Table Answer = 44	**5 x 4** Quick Fire: 4 Times Table Answer = 20
10 x 4 Quick Fire: 4 Times Table Answer = 40	**4 x 4** Quick Fire: 4 Times Table Answer = 16

9 x 4 Quick Fire: 4 Times Table — Answer = 36	**3 x 4** Quick Fire: 4 Times Table — Answer = 12
8 x 4 Quick Fire: 4 Times Table — Answer = 32	**2 x 4** Quick Fire: 4 Times Table — Answer = 8
7 x 4 Quick Fire: 4 Times Table — Answer = 28	**1 x 4** Quick Fire: 4 Times Table — Answer = 4
12 x 5 Quick Fire: 5 Times Table — Answer = 60	**6 x 5** Quick Fire: 5 Times Table — Answer = 30
11 x 5 Quick Fire: 5 Times Table — Answer = 55	**5 x 5** Quick Fire: 5 Times Table — Answer = 25
10 x 5 Quick Fire: 5 Times Table — Answer = 50	**4 x 5** Quick Fire: 5 Times Table — Answer = 20
9 x 5 Quick Fire: 5 Times Table — Answer = 45	**3 x 5** Quick Fire: 5 Times Table — Answer = 15

8 x 5	**2 x 5**
Quick Fire: 5 Times Table Answer = 40	Quick Fire: 5 Times Table Answer = 10
7 x 5	**1 x 5**
Quick Fire: 5 Times Table Answer = 35	Quick Fire: 5 Times Table Answer = 5
12 x 6	**6 x 6**
Quick Fire: 6 Times Table Answer = 72	Quick Fire: 6 Times Table Answer = 36
11 x 6	**5 x 6**
Quick Fire: 6 Times Table Answer = 66	Quick Fire: 6 Times Table Answer = 30
10 x 6	**4 x 6**
Quick Fire: 6 Times Table Answer = 60	Quick Fire: 6 Times Table Answer = 24
9 x 6	**3 x 6**
Quick Fire: 6 Times Table Answer = 54	Quick Fire: 6 Times Table Answer = 18
8 x 6	**2 x 6**
Quick Fire: 6 Times Table Answer = 48	Quick Fire: 6 Times Table Answer = 12

7 x 6	**1 x 6**
Quick Fire: 6 Times Table — Answer = 42	Quick Fire: 6 Times Table — Answer = 6
12 x 7	**6 x 7**
Quick Fire: 7 Times Table — Answer = 84	Quick Fire: 7 Times Table — Answer = 42
11 x 7	**5 x 7**
Quick Fire: 7 Times Table — Answer = 77	Quick Fire: 7 Times Table — Answer = 35
10 x 7	**4 x 7**
Quick Fire: 7 Times Table — Answer = 70	Quick Fire: 7 Times Table — Answer = 28
9 x 7	**3 x 7**
Quick Fire: 7 Times Table — Answer = 63	Quick Fire: 7 Times Table — Answer = 21
8 x 7	**2 x 7**
Quick Fire: 7 Times Table — Answer = 56	Quick Fire: 7 Times Table — Answer = 14
7 x 7	**1 x 7**
Quick Fire: 7 Times Table — Answer = 49	Quick Fire: 7 Times Table — Answer = 7

12 x 8	6 x 8
Quick Fire: 8 Times Table Answer = 96	Quick Fire: 8 Times Table Answer = 48
11 x 8	5 x 8
Quick Fire: 8 Times Table Answer = 88	Quick Fire: 8 Times Table Answer = 40
10 x 8	4 x 8
Quick Fire: 8 Times Table Answer = 80	Quick Fire: 8 Times Table Answer = 32
9 x 8	3 x 8
Quick Fire: 8 Times Table Answer = 72	Quick Fire: 8 Times Table Answer = 24
8 x 8	2 x 8
Quick Fire: 8 Times Table Answer = 64	Quick Fire: 8 Times Table Answer = 16
7 x 8	1 x 8
Quick Fire: 8 Times Table Answer = 56	Quick Fire: 8 Times Table Answer = 8
12 x 9	6 x 9
Quick Fire: 8 Times Table Answer = 108	Quick Fire: 8 Times Table Answer = 54

11 x 9	5 x 9
Quick Fire: 8 Times Table Answer = 99	Quick Fire: 8 Times Table Answer = 45
10 x 9	4 x 9
Quick Fire: 8 Times Table Answer = 90	Quick Fire: 8 Times Table Answer = 36
9 x 9	3 x 9
Quick Fire: 8 Times Table Answer = 81	Quick Fire: 8 Times Table Answer = 27
8 x 9	2 x 9
Quick Fire: 8 Times Table Answer = 72	Quick Fire: 8 Times Table Answer = 18
7 x 9	1 x 9
Quick Fire: 8 Times Table Answer = 63	Quick Fire: 8 Times Table Answer = 9
12 x 10	6 x 10
Quick Fire: 10 Times Table Answer = 12	Quick Fire: 10 Times Table Answer = 60
11 x 10	5 x 10
Quick Fire: 10 Times Table Answer = 110	Quick Fire: 10 Times Table Answer = 50

# 10 x 10	# 4 x 10
Quick Fire: 10 Times Table · Answer = 100	Quick Fire: 10 Times Table · Answer = 40
# 9 x 10	# 3 x 10
Quick Fire: 10 Times Table · Answer = 90	Quick Fire: 10 Times Table · Answer = 30
# 8 x 10	# 2 x 10
Quick Fire: 10 Times Table · Answer = 80	Quick Fire: 10 Times Table · Answer = 20
# 7 x 10	# 1 x 10
Quick Fire: 10 Times Table · Answer = 70	Quick Fire: 10 Times Table · Answer = 10
# 12 x 11	# 6 x 11
Quick Fire: 11 Times Table · Answer = 132	Quick Fire: 11 Times Table · Answer = 66
# 11 x 11	# 5 x 11
Quick Fire: 11 Times Table · Answer = 121	Quick Fire: 11 Times Table · Answer = 55
# 10 x 11	# 4 x 11
Quick Fire: 11 Times Table · Answer = 110	Quick Fire: 11 Times Table · Answer = 44

# 9 x 11	# 3 x 11
Quick Fire: 11 Times Table Answer = 99	Quick Fire: 11 Times Table Answer = 33
# 8 x 11	# 2 x 11
Quick Fire: 11 Times Table Answer = 88	Quick Fire: 11 Times Table Answer = 22
# 7 x 11	# 1 x 11
Quick Fire: 11 Times Table Answer = 77	Quick Fire: 11 Times Table Answer = 110
# 12 x 12	# 6 x 12
Quick Fire: 12 Times Table Answer = 144	Quick Fire: 12 Times Table Answer = 72
# 11 x 12	# 5 x 12
Quick Fire: 12 Times Table Answer = 132	Quick Fire: 12 Times Table Answer = 60
# 10 x 12	# 4 x 12
Quick Fire: 12 Times Table Answer = 120	Quick Fire: 12 Times Table Answer = 48
# 9 x 12	# 3 x 12
Quick Fire: 12 Times Table Answer = 108	Quick Fire: 12 Times Table Answer = 36

# 8 x 12	# 2 x 12
Quick Fire: 12 Times Table Answer = 96	Quick Fire: 12 Times Table Answer = 24
# 7 x 12	# 1 x 12
Quick Fire: 12 Times Table Answer = 84	Quick Fire: 12 Times Table Answer = 12

Activity 7: Multiplication Loop Cards

A game for one or more players

Equipment: Loop Cards and a Stopwatch (optional)

Firstly, photocopy and cut out the cards in one of the sets of Loop Cards from the following pages.

Each pack of loop cards has a set of cards with an answer at the top and a question underneath. The answer to each question is on a different card. The pack of cards are placed face up around the edge of a table. To start the activity, one of the cards is placed at the top of an imaginary circle. The player or players have to then work out the answer to the question on that card. They must then look for the card which has the answer to that question at the top of the card. This card is then placed next to the first card on the imaginary circle. This process is then repeated until the circle or loop is completed. If the loop has been completed correctly, the last card to be placed down should have a question whose answer can be found at the top of the first card.

To make the activity more competitive, each player should try to complete the loop by themselves. While they are doing this, they should be timed using the stopwatch. The winner is the child who completes the loop in the quickest time.

Loop Cards: 1

The answer is 5. The question is... ## 2 x 1 Loop: 1	The answer is 2. The question is... ## 7 x 1 Loop: 1
The answer is 7. The question is... ## 12 x 1 Loop: 1	The answer is 12. The question is... ## 11 x 1 Loop: 1
The answer is 11. The question is... ## 9 x 1 Loop: 1	The answer is 9. The question is... ## 10 x 1 Loop: 1
The answer is 10. The question is... ## 6 x 1 Loop: 1	The answer is 6. The question is... ## 1 x 1 Loop: 1
The answer is 1. The question is... ## 4 x 1 Loop: 1	The answer is 4. The question is... ## 3 x 1 Loop: 1
The answer is 3. The question is... ## 8 x 1 Loop: 1	The answer is 8. The question is... ## 5 x 1 Loop: 1

Loop Cards: 2

The answer is 10. The question is... ## 3 x 2 Loop: 2	The answer is 6. The question is... ## 7 x 2 Loop: 2
The answer is 14. The question is... ## 2 x 2 Loop: 2	The answer is 4. The question is... ## 10 x 2 Loop: 2
The answer is 20. The question is... ## 9 x 2 Loop: 2	The answer is 18. The question is... ## 12 x 2 Loop: 2
The answer is 24. The question is... ## 6 x 2 Loop: 2	The answer is 12. The question is... ## 1 x 2 Loop: 2
The answer is 2. The question is... ## 4 x 2 Loop: 2	The answer is 8. The question is... ## 8 x 2 Loop: 2
The answer is 16. The question is... ## 11 x 2 Loop: 2	The answer is 22. The question is... ## 5 x 2 Loop: 2

Loop Cards: 3

The answer is 3. The question is... **6 x 3** Loop: 3	The answer is 18. The question is... **8 x 3** Loop: 3
The answer is 24. The question is... **9 x 3** Loop: 3	The answer is 27. The question is... **11 x 3** Loop: 3
The answer is 33. The question is... **5 x 3** Loop: 3	The answer is 15. The question is... **7 x 3** Loop: 3
The answer is 21. The question is... **2 x 3** Loop: 3	The answer is 6. The question is... **4 x 3** Loop: 3
The answer is 12. The question is... **10 x 3** Loop: 3	The answer is 30. The question is... **3 x 3** Loop: 3
The answer is 9. The question is... **12 x 3** Loop: 3	The answer is 36. The question is... **1 x 3** Loop: 3

Loop Cards: 4

The answer is 4. The question is…	The answer is 36. The question is…
# 9 x 4	# 6 x 4
Loop: 4	Loop: 4
The answer is 24. The question is…	The answer is 32. The question is…
# 8 x 4	# 10 x 4
Loop: 4	Loop: 4
The answer is 40. The question is…	The answer is 20. The question is…
# 5 x 4	# 2 x 4
Loop: 4	Loop: 4
The answer is 8. The question is…	The answer is 28. The question is…
# 7 x 4	# 4 x 4
Loop: 4	Loop: 4
The answer is 16. The question is…	The answer is 44. The question is…
# 11 x 4	# 3 x 4
Loop: 4	Loop: 4
The answer is 12. The question is…	The answer is 48. The question is…
# 12 x 4	# 1 x 4
Loop: 4	Loop: 4

Loop Cards: 5

The answer is 5. The question is...	The answer is 20. The question is...
# 4 x 5	# 2 x 5
Loop: 5	Loop: 5
The answer is 10. The question is...	The answer is 45. The question is...
# 9 x 5	# 11 x 5
Loop: 5	Loop: 5
The answer is 55. The question is...	The answer is 25. The question is...
# 5 x 5	# 6 x 5
Loop: 5	Loop: 5
The answer is 30. The question is...	The answer is 35. The question is...
# 7 x 5	# 8 x 5
Loop: 5	Loop: 5
The answer is 40. The question is...	The answer is 60. The question is...
# 12 x 5	# 3 x 5
Loop: 5	Loop: 5
The answer is 15. The question is...	The answer is 50. The question is...
# 10 x 5	# 1 x 5
Loop: 5	Loop: 5

Loop Cards: 6

The answer is 18. The question is…	The answer is 12. The question is…
2 x 6	**4 x 6**
Loop: 6	Loop: 6
The answer is 24. The question is…	The answer is 48. The question is…
8 x 6	**10 x 6**
Loop: 6	Loop: 6
The answer is 60. The question is…	The answer is 30. The question is…
5 x 6	**7 x 6**
Loop: 6	Loop: 6
The answer is 42. The question is…	The answer is 36. The question is…
6 x 6	**9 x 6**
Loop: 6	Loop: 6
The answer is 54. The question is…	The answer is 72. The question is…
12 x 6	**1 x 6**
Loop: 6	Loop: 6
The answer is 6. The question is…	The answer is 66. The question is…
11 x 6	**3 x 6**
Loop: 6	Loop: 6

Loop Cards: 7

The answer is 14. The question is… **8 x 7** Loop: 7	The answer is 56. The question is… **4 x 7** Loop: 7
The answer is 28. The question is… **9 x 7** Loop: 7	The answer is 63. The question is… **12 x 7** Loop: 7
The answer is 84. The question is… **5 x 7** Loop: 7	The answer is 35. The question is… **7 x 7** Loop: 7
The answer is 49. The question is… **6 x 7** Loop: 7	The answer is 42. The question is… **3 x 7** Loop: 7
The answer is 21. The question is… **11 x 7** Loop: 7	The answer is 77. The question is… **10 x 7** Loop: 7
The answer is 70. The question is… **1 x 7** Loop: 7	The answer is 7. The question is… **2 x 7** Loop: 7

Loop Cards: 8

The answer is 40. The question is… **1 x 8** Loop: 8	The answer is 8. The question is… **3 x 8** Loop: 8
The answer is 24. The question is… **7 x 8** Loop: 8	The answer is 56. The question is… **10 x 8** Loop: 8
The answer is 80. The question is… **4 x 8** Loop: 8	The answer is 32. The question is… **9 x 8** Loop: 8
The answer is 72. The question is… **6 x 8** Loop: 8	The answer is 48. The question is… **8 x 8** Loop: 8
The answer is 64. The question is… **11 x 8** Loop: 8	The answer is 88. The question is… **12 x 8** Loop: 8
The answer is 96. The question is… **2 x 8** Loop: 8	The answer is 16. The question is… **5 x 8** Loop: 8

Loop Cards: 9

The answer is 72. The question is…	The answer is 36. The question is…
4 x 9 Loop: 9	**5 x 9** Loop: 9
The answer is 45. The question is…	The answer is 9. The question is…
1 x 9 Loop: 9	**10 x 9** Loop: 9
The answer is 90. The question is…	The answer is 18. The question is…
2 x 9 Loop: 9	**11 x 9** Loop: 9
The answer is 99. The question is…	The answer is 63. The question is…
7 x 9 Loop: 9	**9 x 9** Loop: 9
The answer is 81. The question is…	The answer is 108. The question is…
12 x 9 Loop: 9	**6 x 9** Loop: 9
The answer is 54. The question is…	The answer is 27. The question is…
3 x 9 Loop: 9	**8 x 9** Loop: 9

Loop Cards: 10

The answer is 110. The question is…	The answer is 40. The question is…
4 x 10	**8 x 10**
Loop: 10	Loop: 10
The answer is 80. The question is…	The answer is 10. The question is…
1 x 10	**9 x 10**
Loop: 10	Loop: 10
The answer is 90. The question is…	The answer is 50. The question is…
5 x 10	**10 x 10**
Loop: 10	Loop: 10
The answer is 100. The question is…	The answer is 70. The question is…
7 x 10	**3 x 10**
Loop: 10	Loop: 10
The answer is 30. The question is…	The answer is 120. The question is…
12 x 10	**2 x 10**
Loop: 10	Loop: 10
The answer is 20. The question is…	The answer is 60. The question is…
6 x 10	**11 x 10**
Loop: 10	Loop: 10

Loop Cards: 11

The answer is 55. The question is… ## 9 x 11 Loop: 11	The answer is 99. The question is… ## 4 x 11 Loop: 11
The answer is 44. The question is… ## 2 x 11 Loop: 11	The answer is 22. The question is… ## 8 x 11 Loop: 11
The answer is 88. The question is… ## 3 x 11 Loop: 11	The answer is 33. The question is… ## 12 x 11 Loop: 11
The answer is 132. The question is… ## 1 x 11 Loop: 11	The answer is 11. The question is… ## 6 x 11 Loop: 11
The answer is 66. The question is… ## 10 x 11 Loop: 11	The answer is 110. The question is… ## 9 x 11 Loop: 11
The answer is 99. The question is… ## 7 x 11 Loop: 11	The answer is 77. The question is… ## 5 x 11 Loop: 11

Loop Cards: 12

The answer is 120. The question is…	The answer is 36. The question is…
# 3 x 12	# 4 x 12
Loop: 12	Loop: 12
The answer is 48. The question is…	The answer is 108. The question is…
# 9 x 12	# 8 x 12
Loop: 12	Loop: 12
The answer is 96. The question is…	The answer is 24. The question is…
# 2 x 12	# 12 x 12
Loop: 12	Loop: 12
The answer is 144. The question is…	The answer is 60. The question is…
# 5 x 12	# 7 x 12
Loop: 12	Loop: 12
The answer is 84. The question is…	The answer is 132. The question is…
# 11 x 12	# 1 x 12
Loop: 12	Loop: 12
The answer is 12. The question is…	The answer is 72. The question is…
# 6 x 12	# 10 x 12
Loop: 12	Loop: 12

Activity 8: Four In A Row Multiplication

A game for two players

Equipment: Four In A Row Game Card and Counters.

You first need to photocopy and cut out, the Game Card and the individual counters from the following pages.

The aim of the game is to create a straight line of four counters of the same color before your opponent does. The line can run vertically, horizontally, or diagonally. To place a counter on the grid, you must firstly correctly answer the question on the square that you want to cover. Players take it in turns to answer a question. If a player incorrectly answers a question, they cannot place a counter on that square. They can though have a go at answering a different question. Play passes onto their opponent once they have correctly answered one question. The first player to complete a line of counters is the winner.

If necessary, the answers can be checked using the multiplication grid.

3 x 7	2 x 8	3 x 9	2 x 10	7 x 9	8 x 12	4 x 9
2 x 3	4 x 6	5 x 11	7 x 12	4 x 5	2 x 7	2 x 6
2 x 5	6 x 6	5 x 10	9 x 9	8 x 4	9 x 2	11 x 6
4 x 4	6 x 3	7 x 8	4 x 10	11 x 11	3 x 10	7 x 4
6 x 8	5 x 5	6 x 12	5 x 9	8 x 3	9 x 12	5 x 3
9 x 6	11 x 12	8 x 5	3 x 4	6 x 7	8 x 8	12 x 12

Activity 9: Multiplication Tic-Tac-Toe/Noughts and Crosses

There are Tic-Tac-Toe boards, which deal with each of the times tables in turn, on the following pages. Photocopy and cut out, the one that you want to work with and the counters.

The game is similar to the traditional game of tic-tac-toe (called noughts and crosses in Britain) but before children can cover a square on the board, they must first say the multiplication question and give the answer. The first child to complete a straight line of three noughts or crosses is the winner.

If necessary, the answers can be checked using the multiplication grid.

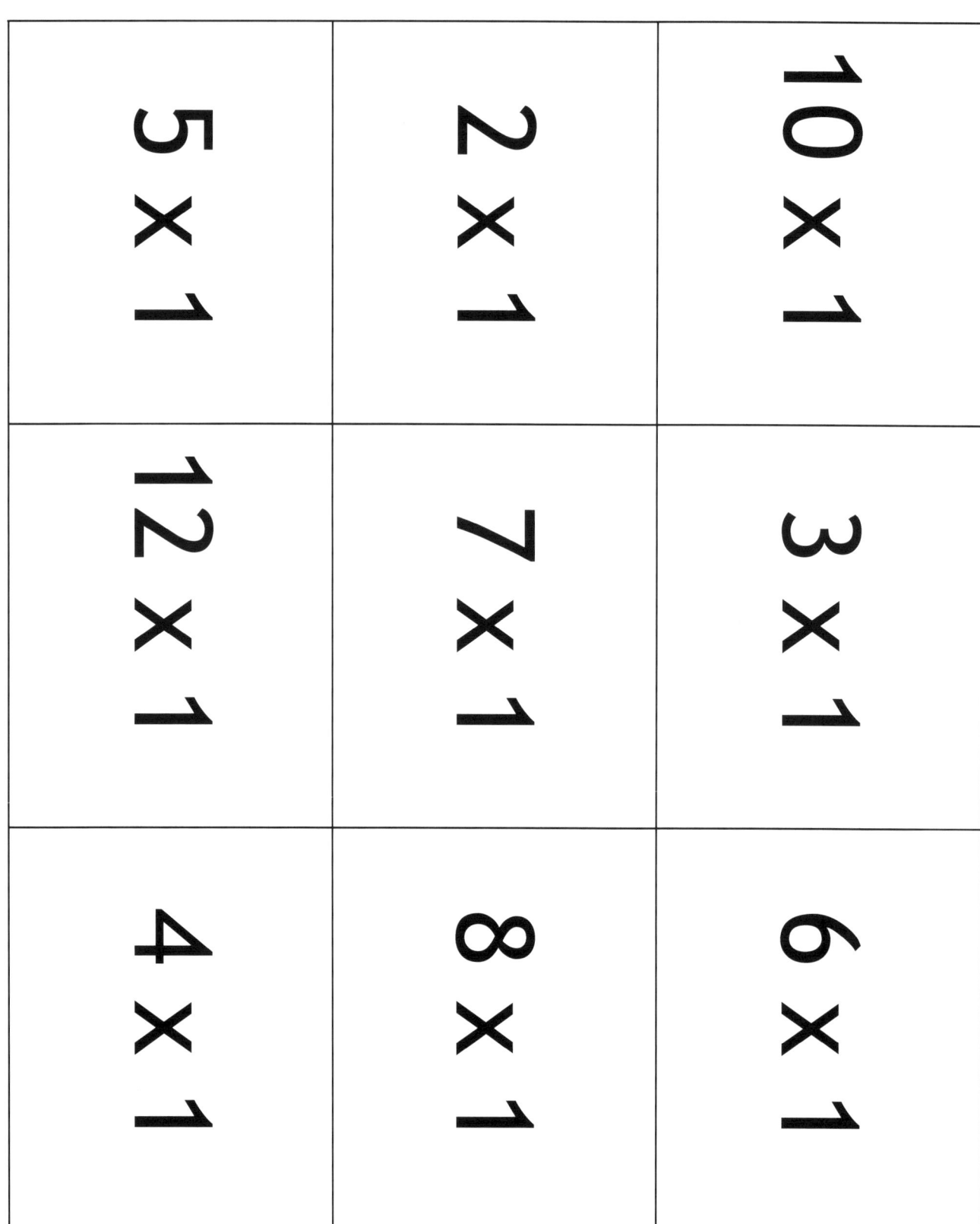

10 x 1	2 x 1	5 x 1
3 x 1	7 x 1	12 x 1
6 x 1	8 x 1	4 x 1

Tic-Tac-Toe/Noughts and Crosses x 1

2 x 2	3 x 2	4 x 2
7 x 2	12 x 2	6 x 2
5 x 2	8 x 2	9 x 2

Tic-Tac-Toe/Noughts and Crosses x 2

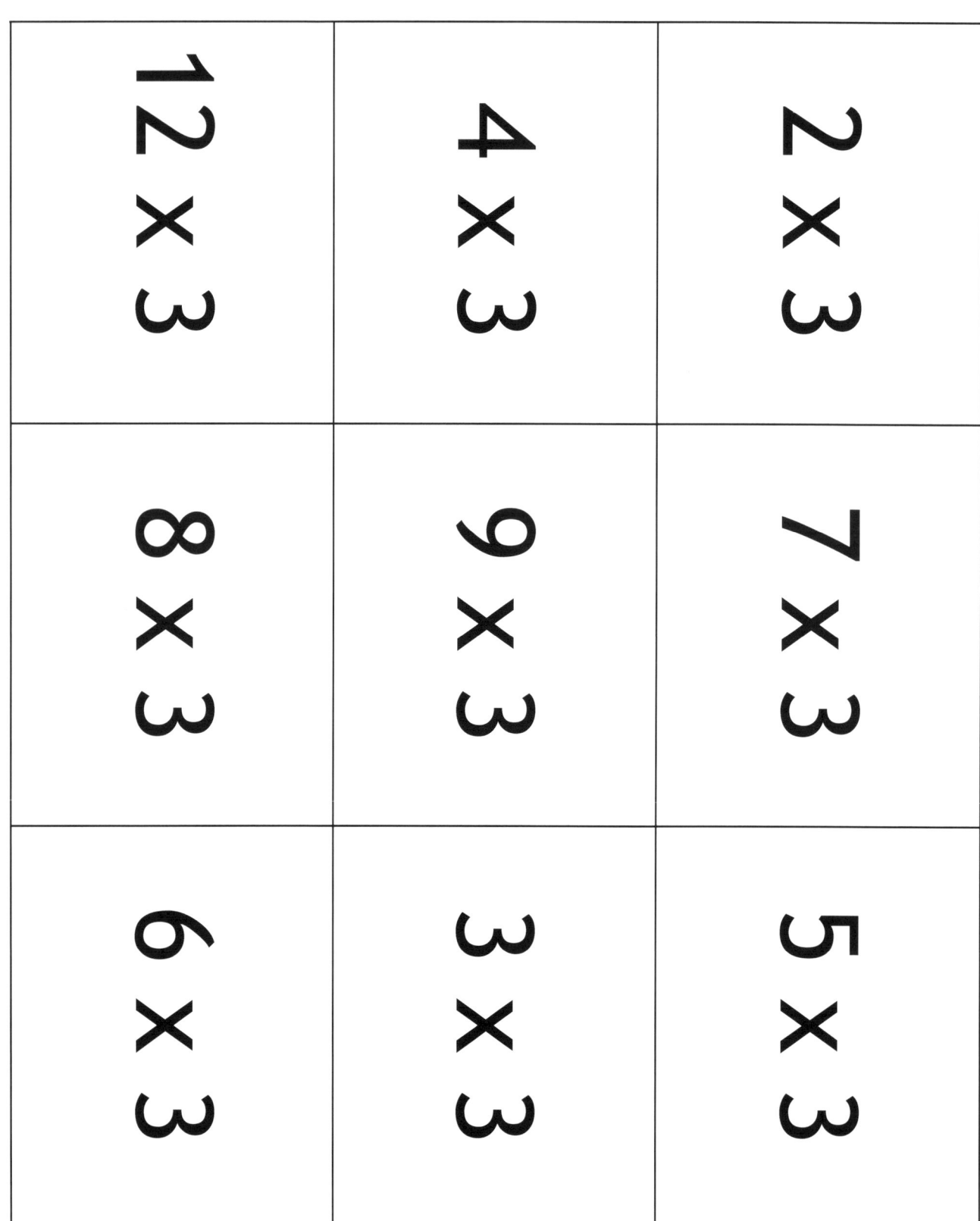

12 x 3	4 x 3	2 x 3
8 x 3	9 x 3	7 x 3
6 x 3	3 x 3	5 x 3

Tic-Tac-Toe/Noughts and Crosses x 3

12 x 4	9 x 4	5 x 4
2 x 4	7 x 4	6 x 4
8 x 4	3 x 4	4 x 4

Tic-Tac-Toe/Noughts and Crosses x 4

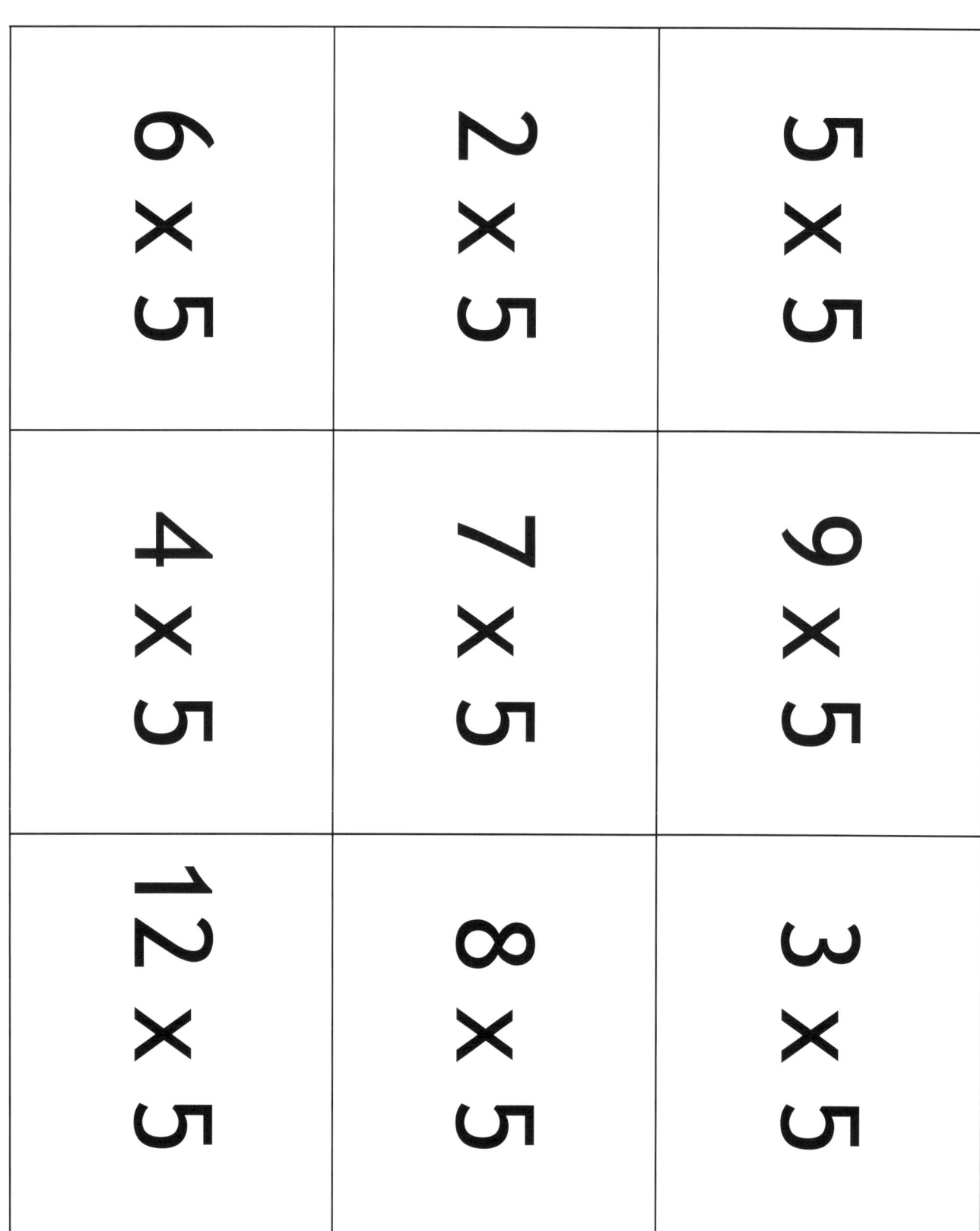

6 x 5	2 x 5	5 x 5
4 x 5	7 x 5	9 x 5
12 x 5	8 x 5	3 x 5

Tic-Tac-Toe/Noughts and Crosses x 5

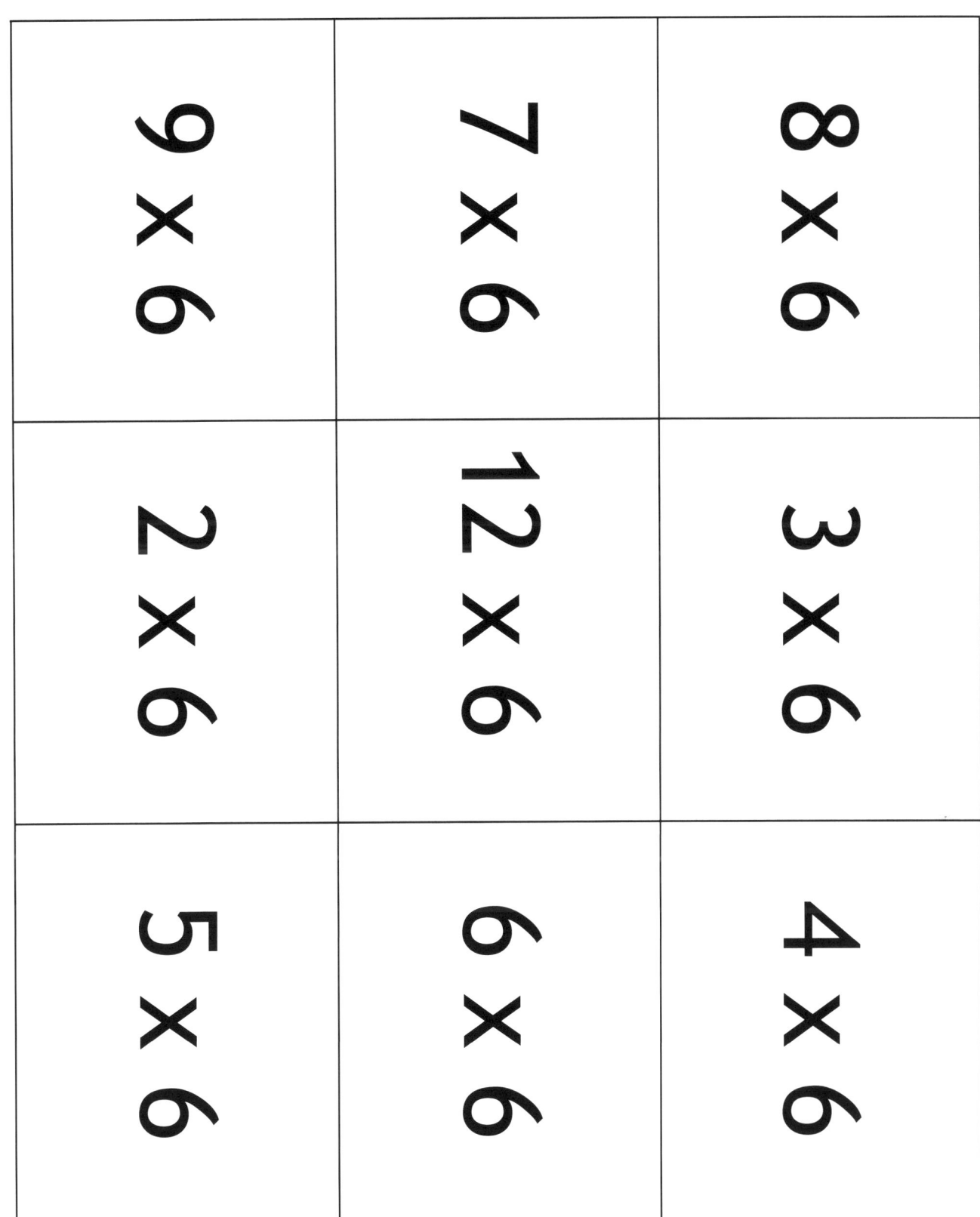

9 x 6

7 x 6

8 x 6

2 x 6

12 x 6

3 x 6

5 x 6

6 x 6

4 x 6

Tic-Tac-Toe/Noughts and Crosses x 6

12 x 7	5 x 7	2 x 7
8 x 7	9 x 7	3 x 7
4 x 7	7 x 7	6 x 7

Tic-Tac-Toe / Noughts and Crosses x 7

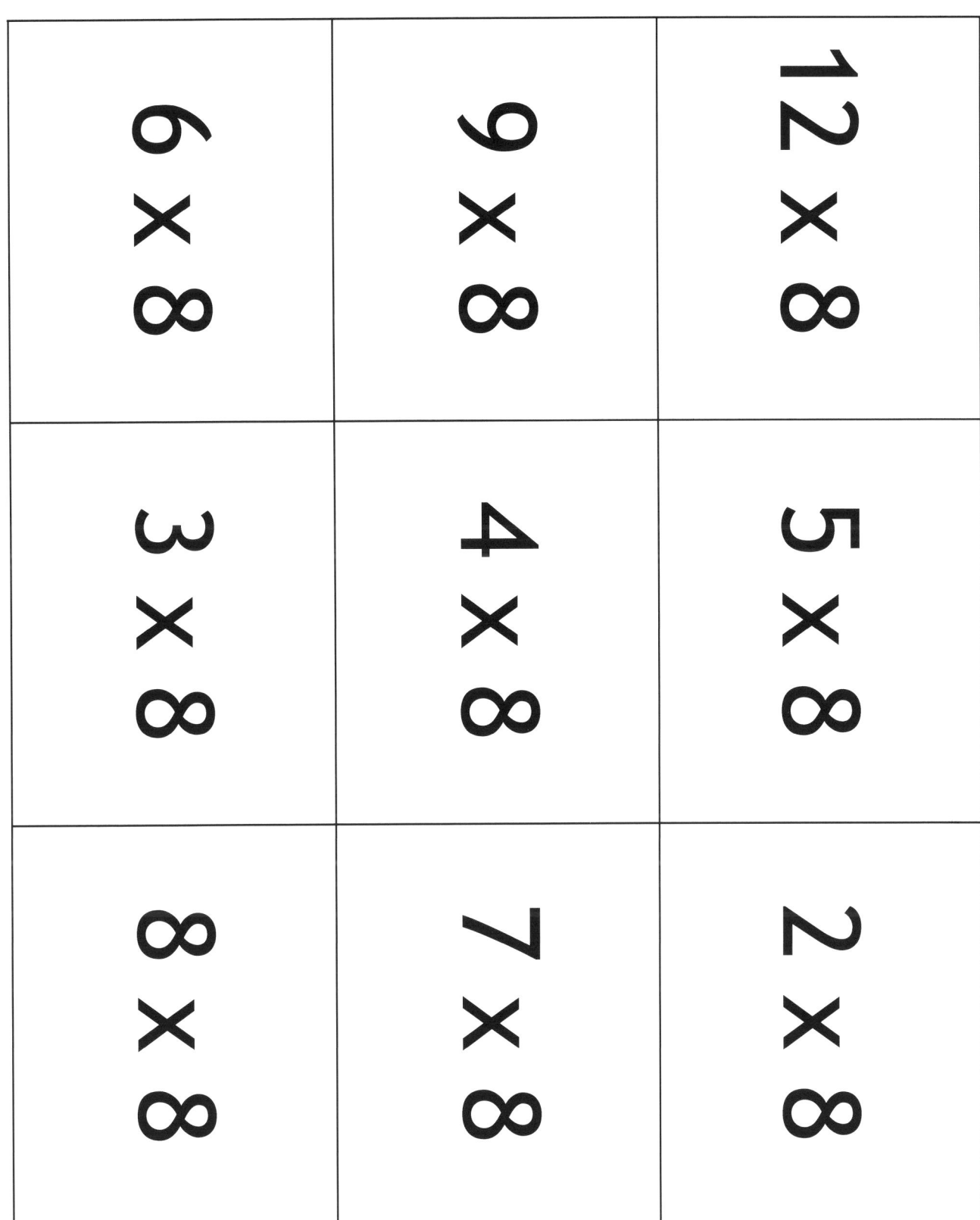

12 x 8	9 x 8	6 x 8
5 x 8	4 x 8	3 x 8
2 x 8	7 x 8	8 x 8

Tic-Tac-Toe/Noughts and Crosses x 8

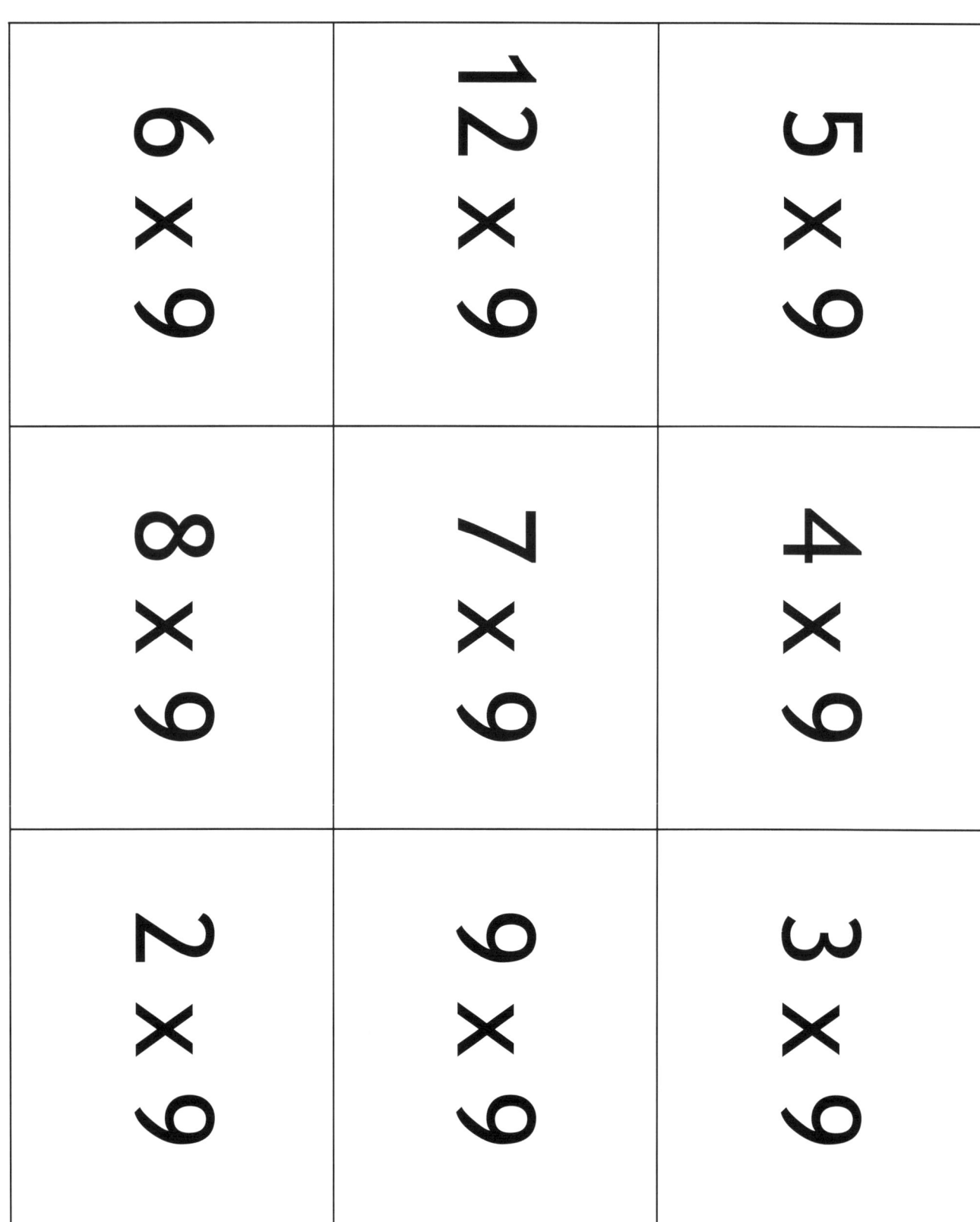

5 x 9	12 x 9	6 x 9
4 x 9	7 x 9	8 x 9
3 x 9	9 x 9	2 x 9

Tic-Tac-Toe/Noughts and Crosses x 9

12 x 10	3 x 10	4 x 10
5 x 10	2 x 10	7 x 10
9 x 10	6 x 10	8 x 10

Tic-Tac-Toe / Noughts and Crosses x 10

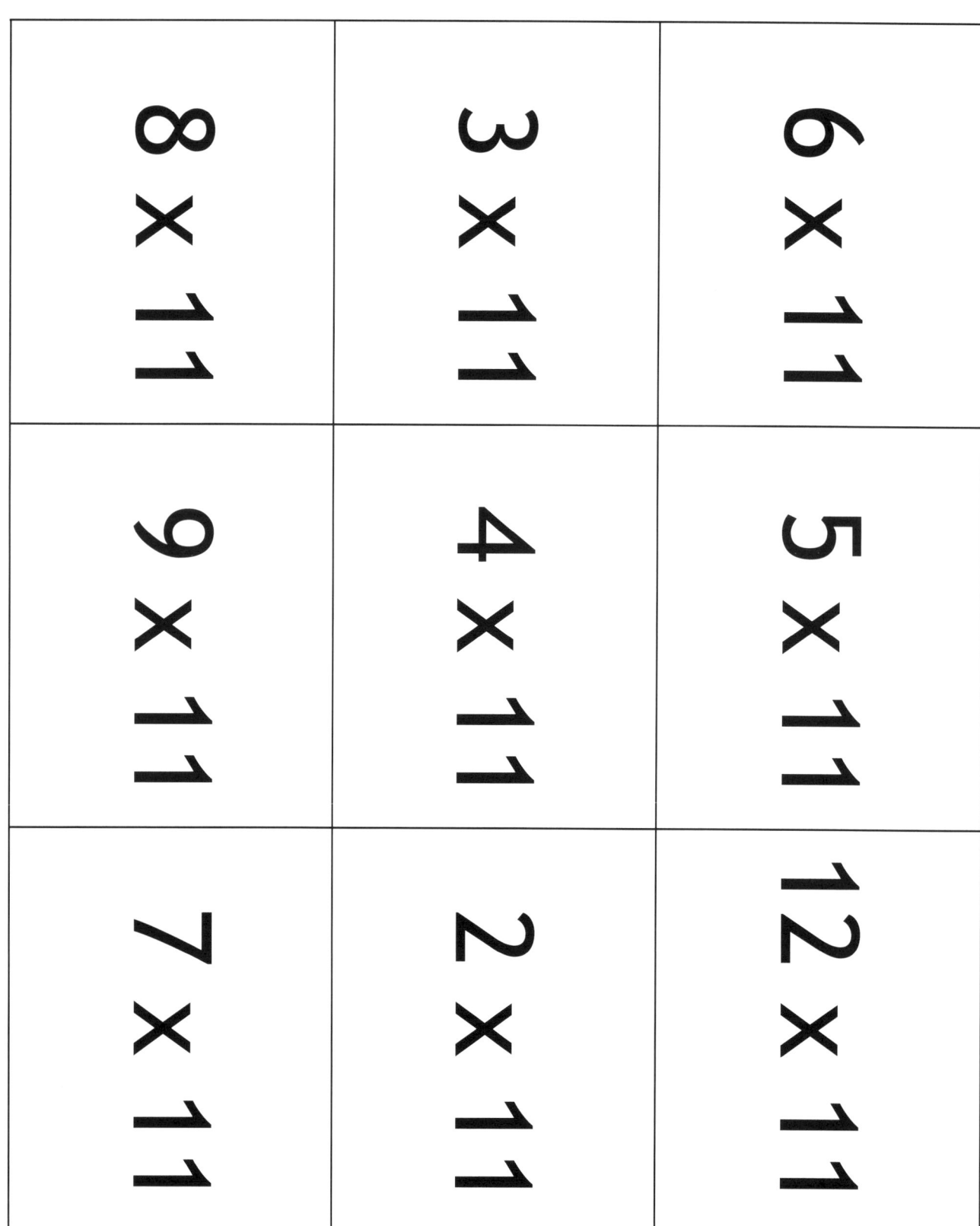

6 x 11	3 x 11	8 x 11
5 x 11	4 x 11	9 x 11
12 x 11	2 x 11	7 x 11

Tic-Tac-Toe/Noughts and Crosses x 11

4 x 12	6 x 12	2 x 12
12 x 12	8 x 12	3 x 12
7 x 12	9 x 12	5 x 12

Tic-Tac-Toe / Noughts and Crosses x 12

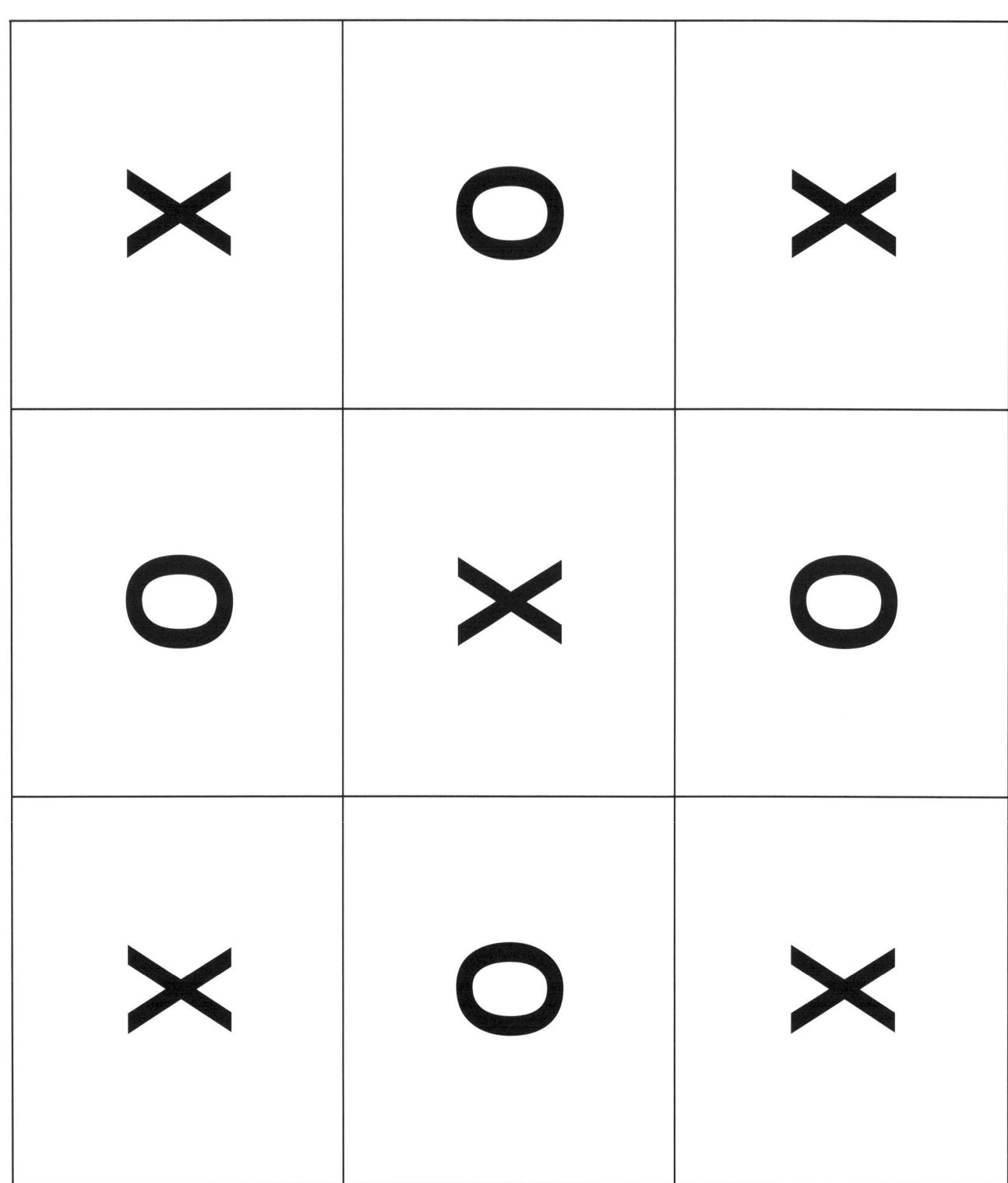

Tic-Tac-Toe/Noughts and Crosses Counters

Activity 10: My Factor

A game for two or more players

Equipment: My Factor Cards, The Multiplication Grid And A Stopwatch

Firstly photocopy and cut out, the question and answer cards for this game from the following pages.

To play the game spread the question cards, face up, on the table. The answer cards should then be placed face down in a pile in the middle of the table. Player one turns over one of the answer cards. They then have 1 minute to find as many question cards as they can which will give the answer on the answer card. Once 1 minute has passed the answer cards are checked to see if they are correct, using the multiplication grid. Each answer card that is correct, earns one point. Each answer card that has incorrectly been picked up, loses one point. Once the score has been worked out, the answer card is placed at the bottom of the pile and the question cards are spread back out on the table. Player two then picks an answer card and repeats the process. The first player to reach 21 points is the winner.

The game can be simplified by removing some of the higher value answer cards and the corresponding question cards.

My Factor Cards

2×2 <small>My Factor: Question</small>	$= 4$ <small>My Factor: Answer</small>
4×1 <small>My Factor: Question</small>	$= 5$ <small>My Factor: Answer</small>
1×4 <small>My Factor: Question</small>	$= 6$ <small>My Factor: Answer</small>
5×1 <small>My Factor: Question</small>	$= 8$ <small>My Factor: Answer</small>
1×5 <small>My Factor: Question</small>	$= 9$ <small>My Factor: Answer</small>
6×1 <small>My Factor: Question</small>	$= 10$ <small>My Factor: Answer</small>
1×6 <small>My Factor: Question</small>	$= 12$ <small>My Factor: Answer</small>

2 x 3	= 14
My Factor: Question	My Factor: Answer
3 x 2	= 15
My Factor: Question	My Factor: Answer
1 x 8	= 16
My Factor: Question	My Factor: Answer
8 x 1	= 18
My Factor: Question	My Factor: Answer
2 x 4	= 20
My Factor: Question	My Factor: Answer
4 x 2	= 24
My Factor: Question	My Factor: Answer
9 x 1	= 28
My Factor: Question	My Factor: Answer

# 1 x 9 My Factor: Question	# = 30 My Factor: Answer
# 3 x 3 My Factor: Question	# = 32 My Factor: Answer
# 5 x 2 My Factor: Question	# = 35 My Factor: Answer
# 10 x 1 My Factor: Question	# 1 x 10 My Factor: Question
# 2 x 5 My Factor: Question	# 2 x 6 My Factor: Question
# 6 x 2 My Factor: Question	# 1 x 12 My Factor: Question
# 12 x 1 My Factor: Question	# 3 x 4 My Factor: Question

4 x 3	2 x 7
My Factor: Question	My Factor: Question
7 x 2	3 x 5
My Factor: Question	My Factor: Question
5 x 3	2 x 8
My Factor: Question	My Factor: Question
8 x 2	4 x 4
My Factor: Question	My Factor: Question
9 x 2	2 x 9
My Factor: Question	My Factor: Question
3 x 6	6 x 3
My Factor: Question	My Factor: Question
4 x 5	5 x 4
My Factor: Question	My Factor: Question

10 x 2 My Factor: Question	**2 x 10** My Factor: Question
2 x 12 My Factor: Question	**12 x 2** My Factor: Question
3 x 8 My Factor: Question	**8 x 3** My Factor: Question
6 x 4 My Factor: Question	**4 x 6** My Factor: Question
4 x 7 My Factor: Question	**7 x 4** My Factor: Question
10 x 3 My Factor: Question	**3 x 10** My Factor: Question
5 x 6 My Factor: Question	**6 x 5** My Factor: Question

# 8 x 4	# 4 x 8
My Factor: Question	My Factor: Question
# 5 x 7	# 7 x 5
My Factor: Question	My Factor: Question

Chapter 3: Times Tables Tests

Within the following chapter there is a series of test questions so that you can formally assess your child's knowledge. To begin with, each test is about one specific times table at a time. The order of the times tables is though mixed up and some of the questions ask for the missing number in a question, for example:

6 x ? = 42

This is to help your child to start forming the link between multiplication and division, which they will need when they begin to divide.

There are also tests which have questions about more than one times table and eventually there is a test on all of the times tables.

It is intended that your child writes down the answers to the questions on a separate piece of paper to avoid you continually having to photocopy the sheets. Initially they should simply attempt to get all of the questions correct. All of the answers are provided so that you can check your child's work with them or so that they can mark it by themselves. Once they can do this confidently, they should then try to improve their speed. They should time how long each test takes with a stopwatch and record their time. Each subsequent time that they try a test, they should try and work more quickly. This element of self-competition should continue to keep your child motivated. The eventual aim should be to finish each set of 48 questions in 5 minutes or less.

The 1 Times Table Test

1) 3 x 1 = ☐   17) 9 x 1 = ☐   33) 10 x 1 = ☐

2) 7 x 1 = ☐   18) 10 x 1 = ☐   34) 6 x 1 = ☐

3) 8 x 1 = ☐   19) 4 x 1 = ☐   35) 12 x 1 = ☐

4) 1 x 1 = ☐   20) 1 x 1 = ☐   36) 11 x 1 = ☐

5) 8 x 1 = ☐   21) 2 x 1 = ☐   37) 4 x 1 = ☐

6) 5 x 1 = ☐   22) 5 x 1 = ☐   38) 7 x 1 = ☐

7) 11 x 1 = ☐   23) 12 x 1 = ☐   39) 9 x 1 = ☐

8) 3 x 1 = ☐   24) 6 x 1 = ☐   40) 2 x 1 = ☐

9) ☐ x 1 = 4   25) ☐ x 1 = 2   41) ☐ x 1 = 12

10) ☐ x 1 = 11   26) ☐ x 1 = 10   42) ☐ x 1 = 9

11) ☐ x 1 = 5   27) ☐ x 1 = 12   43) ☐ x 1 = 2

12) ☐ x 1 = 3   28) ☐ x 1 = 6   44) ☐ x 1 = 3

13) ☐ x 1 = 9   29) ☐ x 1 = 1   45) ☐ x 1 = 6

14) ☐ x 1 = 8   30) ☐ x 1 = 7   46) ☐ x 1 = 8

15) ☐ x 1 = 1   31) ☐ x 1 = 11   47) ☐ x 1 = 10

16) ☐ x 1 = 7   32) ☐ x 1 = 4   48) ☐ x 1 = 5

The 2 Times Table Test

1) 12 x 2 = ☐   17)   6 x 2 = ☐   33)   9 x 2 = ☐

2)   7 x 2 = ☐   18) 10 x 2 = ☐   34)   5 x 2 = ☐

3)   8 x 2 = ☐   19)   4 x 2 = ☐   35) 10 x 2 = ☐

4)   1 x 2 = ☐   20)   6 x 2 = ☐   36) 12 x 2 = ☐

5)   8 x 2 = ☐   21)   2 x 2 = ☐   37)   9 x 2 = ☐

6)   5 x 2 = ☐   22)   3 x 2 = ☐   38) 11 x 2 = ☐

7) 11 x 2 = ☐   23)   7 x 2 = ☐   39)   4 x 2 = ☐

8)   1 x 2 = ☐   24)   3 x 2 = ☐   40)   2 x 2 = ☐

9) ☐ x 2 = 16   25) ☐ x 2 = 20   41) ☐ x 2 = 22

10) ☐ x 2 = 12   26) ☐ x 2 = 24   42) ☐ x 2 = 10

11) ☐ x 2 = 8   27) ☐ x 2 = 18   43) ☐ x 2 = 12

12) ☐ x 2 = 22   28) ☐ x 2 = 6   44) ☐ x 2 = 8

13) ☐ x 2 = 10   29) ☐ x 2 = 16   45) ☐ x 2 = 6

14) ☐ x 2 = 4   30) ☐ x 2 = 20   46) ☐ x 2 = 18

15) ☐ x 2 = 2   31) ☐ x 2 = 14   47) ☐ x 2 = 24

16) ☐ x 2 = 14   32) ☐ x 2 = 4   48) ☐ x 2 = 2

The 1 and 2 Times Tables Test

1)   3 x 2   = ▢   17) 11 x 2   = ▢   33)   8 x 2   = ▢

2)   5 x 1   = ▢   18)   4 x 1   = ▢   34)   7 x 1   = ▢

3)   2 x 2   = ▢   19)   7 x 2   = ▢   35)   6 x 2   = ▢

4)   6 x 1   = ▢   20) 12 x 1   = ▢   36)   2 x 1   = ▢

5)   1 x 2   = ▢   21)   5 x 2   = ▢   37)   9 x 2   = ▢

6)   8 x 1   = ▢   22) 10 x 1   = ▢   38)   9 x 1   = ▢

7) 10 x 2   = ▢   23) 12 x 2   = ▢   39)   4 x 2   = ▢

8)   3 x 1   = ▢   24)   1 x 1   = ▢   40) 11 x 1   = ▢

9) ▢ x 2   = 16   25) ▢ x 2   = 10   41) ▢ x 2   = 24

10) ▢ x 1   =   4   26) ▢ x 1   =   9   42) ▢ x 1   = 11

11) ▢ x 2   =   6   27) ▢ x 2   = 18   43) ▢ x 2   = 22

12) ▢ x 1   = 10   28) ▢ x 1   =   2   44) ▢ x 1   =   5

13) ▢ x 2   = 12   29) ▢ x 2   = 20   45) ▢ x 2   =   4

14) ▢ x 1   = 12   30) ▢ x 1   =   6   46) ▢ x 1   =   7

15) ▢ x 2   =   2   31) ▢ x 2   = 14   47) ▢ x 2   =   8

16) ▢ x 1   =   1   32) ▢ x 1   =   3   48) ▢ x 1   =   8

The 3 Times Table Test

1)	3 x 3 = ☐	17)	9 x 3 = ☐	33)	2 x 3 = ☐
2)	7 x 3 = ☐	18)	10 x 3 = ☐	34)	5 x 3 = ☐
3)	12 x 3 = ☐	19)	5 x 3 = ☐	35)	12 x 3 = ☐
4)	1 x 3 = ☐	20)	6 x 3 = ☐	36)	8 x 3 = ☐
5)	8 x 3 = ☐	21)	2 x 3 = ☐	37)	9 x 3 = ☐
6)	4 x 3 = ☐	22)	6 x 3 = ☐	38)	11 x 3 = ☐
7)	1 x 3 = ☐	23)	7 x 3 = ☐	39)	4 x 3 = ☐
8)	10 x 3 = ☐	24)	3 x 3 = ☐	40)	11 x 3 = ☐
9)	☐ x 3 = 6	25)	☐ x 3 = 30	41)	☐ x 3 = 33
10)	☐ x 3 = 12	26)	☐ x 3 = 24	42)	☐ x 3 = 15
11)	☐ x 3 = 9	27)	☐ x 3 = 18	43)	☐ x 3 = 6
12)	☐ x 3 = 15	28)	☐ x 3 = 33	44)	☐ x 3 = 36
13)	☐ x 3 = 36	29)	☐ x 3 = 24	45)	☐ x 3 = 9
14)	☐ x 3 = 27	30)	☐ x 3 = 27	46)	☐ x 3 = 18
15)	☐ x 3 = 21	31)	☐ x 3 = 21	47)	☐ x 3 = 30
16)	☐ x 3 = 3	32)	☐ x 3 = 3	48)	☐ x 3 = 12

The 4 Times Table Test

1) 6 x 4 = ☐   17) 11 x 4 = ☐   33) 10 x 4 = ☐

2) 7 x 4 = ☐   18) 4 x 4 = ☐   34) 5 x 4 = ☐

3) 12 x 4 = ☐   19) 2 x 4 = ☐   35) 12 x 4 = ☐

4) 10 x 4 = ☐   20) 6 x 4 = ☐   36) 8 x 4 = ☐

5) 8 x 4 = ☐   21) 2 x 4 = ☐   37) 9 x 4 = ☐

6) 9 x 4 = ☐   22) 3 x 4 = ☐   38) 1 x 4 = ☐

7) 1 x 4 = ☐   23) 7 x 4 = ☐   39) 4 x 4 = ☐

8) 5 x 4 = ☐   24) 3 x 4 = ☐   40) 11 x 4 = ☐

9) ☐ x 4 = 12   25) ☐ x 4 = 4   41) ☐ x 4 = 20

10) ☐ x 4 = 20   26) ☐ x 4 = 16   42) ☐ x 4 = 12

11) ☐ x 4 = 44   27) ☐ x 4 = 8   43) ☐ x 4 = 40

12) ☐ x 4 = 28   28) ☐ x 4 = 40   44) ☐ x 4 = 36

13) ☐ x 4 = 36   29) ☐ x 4 = 4   45) ☐ x 4 = 8

14) ☐ x 4 = 32   30) ☐ x 4 = 24   46) ☐ x 4 = 16

15) ☐ x 4 = 24   31) ☐ x 4 = 48   47) ☐ x 4 = 32

16) ☐ x 4 = 48   32) ☐ x 4 = 28   48) ☐ x 4 = 44

97

The 3 and 4 Times Tables Test

1) 5 x 4 = ☐   17) 1 x 4 = ☐   33) 2 x 4 = ☐

2) 7 x 3 = ☐   18) 12 x 3 = ☐   34) 3 x 3 = ☐

3) 12 x 4 = ☐   19) 9 x 4 = ☐   35) 8 x 4 = ☐

4) 2 x 3 = ☐   20) 1 x 3 = ☐   36) 1 x 3 = ☐

5) 3 x 4 = ☐   21) 7 x 4 = ☐   37) 4 x 4 = ☐

6) 5 x 3 = ☐   22) 10 x 3 = ☐   38) 6 x 3 = ☐

7) 11 x 4 = ☐   23) 10 x 4 = ☐   39) 6 x 4 = ☐

8) 9 x 3 = ☐   24) 8 x 3 = ☐   40) 11 x 3 = ☐

9) ☐ x 4 = 16   25) ☐ x 4 = 32   41) ☐ x 4 = 24

10) ☐ x 3 = 33   26) ☐ x 3 = 9   42) ☐ x 3 = 15

11) ☐ x 4 = 4   27) ☐ x 4 = 20   43) ☐ x 4 = 44

12) ☐ x 3 = 18   28) ☐ x 3 = 24   44) ☐ x 3 = 36

13) ☐ x 4 = 12   29) ☐ x 4 = 28   45) ☐ x 4 = 8

14) ☐ x 3 = 3   30) ☐ x 3 = 6   46) ☐ x 3 = 27

15) ☐ x 4 = 40   31) ☐ x 4 = 48   47) ☐ x 4 = 36

16) ☐ x 3 = 30   32) ☐ x 3 = 21   48) ☐ x 3 = 12

The 1, 2, 3 and 4 Times Tables Test

1) 4 x 1 = ☐
2) 6 x 2 = ☐
3) 12 x 3 = ☐
4) 10 x 4 = ☐
5) 6 x 1 = ☐
6) 8 x 2 = ☐
7) 1 x 3 = ☐
8) 5 x 4 = ☐
9) ☐ x 1 = 10
10) ☐ x 2 = 14
11) ☐ x 3 = 30
12) ☐ x 4 = 28
13) ☐ x 1 = 9
14) ☐ x 2 = 2
15) ☐ x 3 = 24
16) ☐ x 4 = 48

17) 12 x 1 = ☐
18) 5 x 2 = ☐
19) 2 x 3 = ☐
20) 6 x 4 = ☐
21) 1 x 1 = ☐
22) 3 x 2 = ☐
23) 7 x 3 = ☐
24) 3 x 4 = ☐
25) ☐ x 1 = 7
26) ☐ x 2 = 18
27) ☐ x 3 = 9
28) ☐ x 4 = 16
29) ☐ x 1 = 2
30) ☐ x 2 = 24
31) ☐ x 3 = 18
32) ☐ x 4 = 32

33) 11 x 1 = ☐
34) 2 x 2 = ☐
35) 11 x 3 = ☐
36) 1 x 4 = ☐
37) 3 x 1 = ☐
38) 4 x 2 = ☐
39) 4 x 3 = ☐
40) 11 x 4 = ☐
41) ☐ x 1 = 5
42) ☐ x 2 = 22
43) ☐ x 3 = 27
44) ☐ x 4 = 36
45) ☐ x 1 = 8
46) ☐ x 2 = 20
47) ☐ x 3 = 15
48) ☐ x 4 = 8

The 5 Times Table Test

1) 9 x 5 = ☐   17) 2 x 5 = ☐   33) 10 x 5 = ☐

2) 7 x 5 = ☐   18) 4 x 5 = ☐   34) 3 x 5 = ☐

3) 12 x 5 = ☐   19) 2 x 5 = ☐   35) 12 x 5 = ☐

4) 5 x 5 = ☐   20) 6 x 5 = ☐   36) 8 x 5 = ☐

5) 8 x 5 = ☐   21) 7 x 5 = ☐   37) 9 x 5 = ☐

6) 11 x 5 = ☐   22) 3 x 5 = ☐   38) 1 x 5 = ☐

7) 10 x 5 = ☐   23) 5 x 5 = ☐   39) 4 x 5 = ☐

8) 1 x 5 = ☐   24) 6 x 5 = ☐   40) 11 x 5 = ☐

9) ☐ x 5 = 30   25) ☐ x 5 = 5   41) ☐ x 5 = 20

10) ☐ x 5 = 20   26) ☐ x 5 = 15   42) ☐ x 5 = 50

11) ☐ x 5 = 10   27) ☐ x 5 = 25   43) ☐ x 5 = 25

12) ☐ x 5 = 35   28) ☐ x 5 = 55   44) ☐ x 5 = 30

13) ☐ x 5 = 50   29) ☐ x 5 = 5   45) ☐ x 5 = 55

14) ☐ x 5 = 60   30) ☐ x 5 = 60   46) ☐ x 5 = 15

15) ☐ x 5 = 45   31) ☐ x 5 = 45   47) ☐ x 5 = 35

16) ☐ x 5 = 40   32) ☐ x 5 = 10   48) ☐ x 5 = 40

The 6 Times Table Test

1) 9 x 6 = ☐

2) 4 x 6 = ☐

3) 11 x 6 = ☐

4) 5 x 6 = ☐

5) 8 x 6 = ☐

6) 10 x 6 = ☐

7) 2 x 6 = ☐

8) 1 x 6 = ☐

9) ☐ x 6 = 24

10) ☐ x 6 = 60

11) ☐ x 6 = 18

12) ☐ x 6 = 36

13) ☐ x 6 = 72

14) ☐ x 6 = 30

15) ☐ x 6 = 54

16) ☐ x 6 = 48

17) 6 x 6 = ☐

18) 4 x 6 = ☐

19) 2 x 6 = ☐

20) 6 x 6 = ☐

21) 7 x 6 = ☐

22) 3 x 6 = ☐

23) 10 x 6 = ☐

24) 8 x 6 = ☐

25) ☐ x 6 = 12

26) ☐ x 6 = 42

27) ☐ x 6 = 72

28) ☐ x 6 = 6

29) ☐ x 6 = 66

30) ☐ x 6 = 6

31) ☐ x 6 = 42

32) ☐ x 6 = 12

33) 12 x 6 = ☐

34) 3 x 6 = ☐

35) 11 x 6 = ☐

36) 1 x 6 = ☐

37) 9 x 6 = ☐

38) 5 x 6 = ☐

39) 7 x 6 = ☐

40) 12 x 6 = ☐

41) ☐ x 6 = 24

42) ☐ x 6 = 60

43) ☐ x 6 = 18

44) ☐ x 6 = 30

45) ☐ x 6 = 72

46) ☐ x 6 = 36

47) ☐ x 6 = 54

48) ☐ x 6 = 48

The 5 and 6 Times Tables Test

1) 3 x 6 = ☐   17) 5 x 6 = ☐   33) 2 x 6 = ☐

2) 9 x 5 = ☐   18) 10 x 5 = ☐   34) 5 x 5 = ☐

3) 10 x 6 = ☐   19) 8 x 6 = ☐   35) 1 x 6 = ☐

4) 6 x 5 = ☐   20) 4 x 5 = ☐   36) 8 x 5 = ☐

5) 7 x 6 = ☐   21) 9 x 6 = ☐   37) 6 x 6 = ☐

6) 2 x 5 = ☐   22) 11 x 5 = ☐   38) 7 x 5 = ☐

7) 12 x 6 = ☐   23) 11 x 6 = ☐   39) 4 x 6 = ☐

8) 12 x 5 = ☐   24) 1 x 5 = ☐   40) 3 x 5 = ☐

9) ☐ x 6 = 12   25) ☐ x 6 = 30   41) ☐ x 6 = 24

10) ☐ x 5 = 55   26) ☐ x 5 = 10   42) ☐ x 5 = 50

11) ☐ x 6 = 6   27) ☐ x 6 = 18   43) ☐ x 6 = 54

12) ☐ x 5 = 5   28) ☐ x 5 = 25   44) ☐ x 5 = 60

13) ☐ x 6 = 66   29) ☐ x 6 = 72   45) ☐ x 6 = 48

14) ☐ x 5 = 30   30) ☐ x 5 = 45   46) ☐ x 5 = 15

15) ☐ x 6 = 60   31) ☐ x 6 = 42   47) ☐ x 6 = 36

16) ☐ x 5 = 40   32) ☐ x 5 = 20   48) ☐ x 5 = 35

The 1, 2, 3, 4, 5 and 6 Times Tables Test

1) 8 x 6 = ☐   17) 9 x 2 = ☐   33) 4 x 4 = ☐

2) 7 x 5 = ☐   18) 11 x 1 = ☐   34) 7 x 3 = ☐

3) 11 x 4 = ☐   19) 9 x 6 = ☐   35) 7 x 2 = ☐

4) 6 x 3 = ☐   20) 8 x 5 = ☐   36) 8 x 1 = ☐

5) 8 x 2 = ☐   21) 9 x 4 = ☐   37) 4 x 6 = ☐

6) 9 x 1 = ☐   22) 12 x 3 = ☐   38) 5 x 5 = ☐

7) 10 x 6 = ☐   23) 10 x 2 = ☐   39) 8 x 4 = ☐

8) 12 x 5 = ☐   24) 5 x 1 = ☐   40) 10 x 3 = ☐

9) ☐ x 4 = 20   25) ☐ x 6 = 42   41) ☐ x 2 = 66

10) ☐ x 3 = 9   26) ☐ x 5 = 55   42) ☐ x 1 = 50

11) ☐ x 2 = 10 27) ☐ x 4 = 28   43) ☐ x 6 = 24

12) ☐ x 1 = 7   28) ☐ x 3 = 27   44) ☐ x 5 = 22

13) ☐ x 6 = 72 29) ☐ x 2 = 12   45) ☐ x 4 = 24

14) ☐ x 5 = 30 30) ☐ x 1 = 12   46) ☐ x 3 = 33

15) ☐ x 4 = 8   31) ☐ x 6 = 36   47) ☐ x 2 = 48

16) ☐ x 3 = 15 32) ☐ x 5 = 20   48) ☐ x 1 = 30

The 7 Times Tables Test

1) 4 x 7 = ☐   17) 6 x 7 = ☐   33) 10 x 7 = ☐

2) 3 x 7 = ☐   18) 4 x 7 = ☐   34) 9 x 7 = ☐

3) 12 x 7 = ☐   19) 2 x 7 = ☐   35) 11 x 7 = ☐

4) 5 x 7 = ☐   20) 6 x 7 = ☐   36) 12 x 7 = ☐

5) 7 x 7 = ☐   21) 9 x 7 = ☐   37) 8 x 7 = ☐

6) 10 x 7 = ☐   22) 3 x 7 = ☐   38) 5 x 7 = ☐

7) 2 x 7 = ☐   23) 11 x 7 = ☐   39) 7 x 7 = ☐

8) 1 x 7 = ☐   24) 8 x 7 = ☐   40) 1 x 7 = ☐

9) ☐ x 7 = 49   25) ☐ x 7 = 21   41) ☐ x 7 = 28

10) ☐ x 7 = 84   26) ☐ x 7 = 7   42) ☐ x 7 = 7

11) ☐ x 7 = 42   27) ☐ x 7 = 28   43) ☐ x 7 = 77

12) ☐ x 7 = 70   28) ☐ x 7 = 77   44) ☐ x 7 = 63

13) ☐ x 7 = 35   29) ☐ x 7 = 56   45) ☐ x 7 = 14

14) ☐ x 7 = 14   30) ☐ x 7 = 49   46) ☐ x 7 = 35

15) ☐ x 7 = 56   31) ☐ x 7 = 42   47) ☐ x 7 = 84

16) ☐ x 7 = 63   32) ☐ x 7 = 21   48) ☐ x 7 = 70

The 8 Times Tables Test

1) 4 x 8 = ☐   17) 8 x 8 = ☐   33) 10 x 8 = ☐

2) 9 x 8 = ☐   18) 4 x 8 = ☐   34) 2 x 8 = ☐

3) 12 x 8 = ☐   19) 2 x 8 = ☐   35) 10 x 8 = ☐

4) 5 x 8 = ☐   20) 6 x 8 = ☐   36) 12 x 8 = ☐

5) 7 x 8 = ☐   21) 3 x 8 = ☐   37) 11 x 8 = ☐

6) 1 x 8 = ☐   22) 9 x 8 = ☐   38) 5 x 8 = ☐

7) 6 x 8 = ☐   23) 3 x 8 = ☐   39) 7 x 8 = ☐

8) 11 x 8 = ☐   24) 8 x 8 = ☐   40) 1 x 8 = ☐

9) ☐ x 8 = 24   25) ☐ x 8 = 88   41) ☐ x 8 = 32

10) ☐ x 8 = 80   26) ☐ x 8 = 48   42) ☐ x 8 = 56

11) ☐ x 8 = 56   27) ☐ x 8 = 40   43) ☐ x 8 = 24

12) ☐ x 8 = 96   28) ☐ x 8 = 72   44) ☐ x 8 = 88

13) ☐ x 8 = 16   29) ☐ x 8 =   8   45) ☐ x 8 = 16

14) ☐ x 8 =   8   30) ☐ x 8 = 48   46) ☐ x 8 = 40

15) ☐ x 8 = 32   31) ☐ x 8 = 96   47) ☐ x 8 = 64

16) ☐ x 8 = 64   32) ☐ x 8 = 80   48) ☐ x 8 = 72

The 7 and Times Table Test

1) 8 x 8 = ☐ 17) 3 x 8 = ☐ 33) 4 x 8 = ☐

2) 4 x 7 = ☐ 18) 12 x 7 = ☐ 34) 8 x 7 = ☐

3) 10 x 8 = ☐ 19) 2 x 8 = ☐ 35) 1 x 8 = ☐

4) 9 x 7 = ☐ 20) 6 x 7 = ☐ 36) 3 x 7 = ☐

5) 5 x 8 = ☐ 21) 7 x 8 = ☐ 37) 9 x 8 = ☐

6) 1 x 7 = ☐ 22) 10 x 7 = ☐ 38) 5 x 7 = ☐

7) 12 x 8 = ☐ 23) 11 x 8 = ☐ 39) 6 x 8 = ☐

8) 11 x 7 = ☐ 24) 2 x 7 = ☐ 40) 7 x 7 = ☐

9) ☐ x 8 = 8 25) ☐ x 8 = 32 41) ☐ x 8 = 24

10) ☐ x 7 = 35 26) ☐ x 7 = 21 42) ☐ x 7 = 42

11) ☐ x 8 = 16 27) ☐ x 8 = 80 43) ☐ x 8 = 48

12) ☐ x 7 = 14 28) ☐ x 7 = 28 44) ☐ x 7 = 63

13) ☐ x 8 = 64 29) ☐ x 8 = 72 45) ☐ x 8 = 88

14) ☐ x 7 = 84 30) ☐ x 7 = 56 46) ☐ x 7 = 7

15) ☐ x 8 = 56 31) ☐ x 8 = 40 47) ☐ x 8 = 96

16) ☐ x 7 = 77 32) ☐ x 7 = 70 48) ☐ x 7 = 49

The 5, 6, 7 and 8 Times Tables Test

1) 3 x 5 = ☐   17) 10 x 5 = ☐   33) 6 x 5 = ☐

2) 9 x 6 = ☐   18) 8 x 6 = ☐   34) 7 x 6 = ☐

3) 11 x 7 = ☐   19) 2 x 7 = ☐   35) 9 x 7 = ☐

4) 10 x 8 = ☐   20) 8 x 8 = ☐   36) 1 x 8 = ☐

5) 9 x 5 = ☐   21) 11 x 5 = ☐   37) 5 x 5 = ☐

6) 2 x 6 = ☐   22) 3 x 6 = ☐   38) 11 x 6 = ☐

7) 1 x 7 = ☐   23) 7 x 7 = ☐   39) 10 x 7 = ☐

8) 5 x 8 = ☐   24) 2 x 8 = ☐   40) 11 x 8 = ☐

9) ☐ x 5 = 5   25) ☐ x 5 = 35   41) ☐ x 5 = 40

10) ☐ x 6 = 24   26) ☐ x 6 = 36   42) ☐ x 6 = 72

11) ☐ x 7 = 35   27) ☐ x 7 = 56   43) ☐ x 7 = 84

12) ☐ x 8 = 24   28) ☐ x 8 = 56   44) ☐ x 8 = 72

13) ☐ x 5 = 10   29) ☐ x 5 = 20   45) ☐ x 5 = 60

14) ☐ x 6 = 6   30) ☐ x 6 = 60   46) ☐ x 6 = 30

15) ☐ x 7 = 28   31) ☐ x 7 = 21   47) ☐ x 7 = 42

16) ☐ x 8 = 48   32) ☐ x 8 = 32   48) ☐ x 8 = 96

The 9 Times Table Test

1) 1 x 9 = ⬜

2) 6 x 9 = ⬜

3) 10 x 9 = ⬜

4) 5 x 9 = ⬜

5) 9 x 9 = ⬜

6) 4 x 9 = ⬜

7) 6 x 9 = ⬜

8) 12 x 9 = ⬜

9) ⬜ x 9 = 18

10) ⬜ x 9 = 45

11) ⬜ x 9 = 54

12) ⬜ x 9 = 108

13) ⬜ x 9 = 99

14) ⬜ x 9 = 9

15) ⬜ x 9 = 27

16) ⬜ x 9 = 63

17) 8 x 9 = ⬜

18) 4 x 9 = ⬜

19) 2 x 9 = ⬜

20) 7 x 9 = ⬜

21) 2 x 9 = ⬜

22) 9 x 9 = ⬜

23) 3 x 9 = ⬜

24) 8 x 9 = ⬜

25) ⬜ x 9 = 72

26) ⬜ x 9 = 36

27) ⬜ x 9 = 90

28) ⬜ x 9 = 81

29) ⬜ x 9 = 45

30) ⬜ x 9 = 9

31) ⬜ x 9 = 108

32) ⬜ x 9 = 81

33) 11 x 9 = ⬜

34) 3 x 9 = ⬜

35) 12 x 9 = ⬜

36) 11 x 9 = ⬜

37) 10 x 9 = ⬜

38) 5 x 9 = ⬜

39) 7 x 9 = ⬜

40) 1 x 9 = ⬜

41) ⬜ x 9 = 36

42) ⬜ x 9 = 54

43) ⬜ x 9 = 27

44) ⬜ x 9 = 90

45) ⬜ x 9 = 18

46) ⬜ x 9 = 99

47) ⬜ x 9 = 63

48) ⬜ x 9 = 72

The 10 Times Table Test

1) 12 x 10 = ☐

2) 7 x 10 = ☐

3) 10 x 10 = ☐

4) 2 x 10 = ☐

5) 8 x 10 = ☐

6) 4 x 10 = ☐

7) 12 x 10 = ☐

8) 10 x 10 = ☐

9) ☐ x 10 = 50

10) ☐ x 10 = 40

11) ☐ x 10 = 10

12) ☐ x 10 = 20

13) ☐ x 10 = 60

14) ☐ x 10 = 90

15) ☐ x 10 = 70

16) ☐ x 10 = 80

17) 1 x 10 = ☐

18) 11 x 10 = ☐

19) 4 x 10 = ☐

20) 5 x 10 = ☐

21) 6 x 10 = ☐

22) 11 x 10 = ☐

23) 9 x 10 = ☐

24) 3 x 10 = ☐

25) ☐ x 10 = 120

26) ☐ x 10 = 60

27) ☐ x 10 = 30

28) ☐ x 10 = 110

29) ☐ x 10 = 70

30) ☐ x 10 = 40

31) ☐ x 10 = 110

32) ☐ x 10 = 10

33) 2 x 10 = ☐

34) 7 x 10 = ☐

35) 3 x 10 = ☐

36) 9 x 10 = ☐

37) 8 x 10 = ☐

38) 1 x 10 = ☐

39) 5 x 10 = ☐

40) 6 x 10 = ☐

41) ☐ x 10 = 50

42) ☐ x 10 = 30

43) ☐ x 10 = 80

44) ☐ x 10 = 90

45) ☐ x 10 = 100

46) ☐ x 10 = 20

47) ☐ x 10 = 100

48) ☐ x 10 = 120

The 9 and 10 Times Table Test

1) 12 x 10 = ☐   17) 1 x 10 = ☐   33) 2 x 10 = ☐

2) 7 x 9 = ☐   18) 11 x 9 = ☐   34) 8 x 9 = ☐

3) 10 x 10 = ☐   19) 4 x 10 = ☐   35) 3 x 10 = ☐

4) 5 x 9 = ☐   20) 2 x 9 = ☐   36) 9 x 9 = ☐

5) 7 x 10 = ☐   21) 6 x 10 = ☐   37) 8 x 10 = ☐

6) 1 x 9 = ☐   22) 12 x 9 = ☐   38) 4 x 9 = ☐

7) 11 x 10 = ☐   23) 9 x 10 = ☐   39) 5 x 10 = ☐

8) 10 x 9 = ☐   24) 3 x 9 = ☐   40) 6 x 9 = ☐

9) ☐ x 10 = 50   25) ☐ x 10 = 120   41) ☐ x 10 = 40

10) ☐ x 9 = 36   26) ☐ x 9 = 54   42) ☐ x 9 = 27

11) ☐ x 10 = 10   27) ☐ x 10 = 80   43) ☐ x 10 = 30

12) ☐ x 9 = 18   28) ☐ x 9 = 108   44) ☐ x 9 = 90

13) ☐ x 10 = 60   29) ☐ x 10 = 70   45) ☐ x 10 = 100

14) ☐ x 9 = 81   30) ☐ x 9 = 45   46) ☐ x 9 = 63

15) ☐ x 10 = 20   31) ☐ x 10 = 110   47) ☐ x 10 = 90

16) ☐ x 9 = 72   32) ☐ x 9 = 9   48) ☐ x 9 = 99

The 11 Times Table Test

1) 9 x 11 = ☐
2) 6 x 11 = ☐
3) 10 x 11 = ☐
4) 8 x 11 = ☐
5) 10 x 11 = ☐
6) 4 x 11 = ☐
7) 7 x 11 = ☐
8) 12 x 11 = ☐
9) ☐ x 11 = 33
10) ☐ x 11 = 66
11) ☐ x 11 = 121
12) ☐ x 11 = 110
13) ☐ x 11 = 121
14) ☐ x 11 = 77
15) ☐ x 11 = 55
16) ☐ x 11 = 132

17) 2 x 11 = ☐
18) 4 x 11 = ☐
19) 3 x 11 = ☐
20) 7 x 11 = ☐
21) 8 x 11 = ☐
22) 9 x 11 = ☐
23) 3 x 11 = ☐
24) 6 x 11 = ☐
25) ☐ x 11 = 88
26) ☐ x 11 = 99
27) ☐ x 11 = 132
28) ☐ x 11 = 55
29) ☐ x 11 = 44
30) ☐ x 11 = 110
31) ☐ x 11 = 99
32) ☐ x 11 = 22

33) 1 x 11 = ☐
34) 5 x 11 = ☐
35) 12 x 11 = ☐
36) 11 x 11 = ☐
37) 5 x 11 = ☐
38) 1 x 11 = ☐
39) 11 x 11 = ☐
40) 2 x 11 = ☐
41) ☐ x 11 = 44
42) ☐ x 11 = 77
43) ☐ x 11 = 22
44) ☐ x 11 = 11
45) ☐ x 11 = 88
46) ☐ x 11 = 33
47) ☐ x 11 = 11
48) ☐ x 11 = 66

The 12 Times Table Test

1) 9 x 12 = ☐   17) 8 x 12 = ☐   33) 1 x 12 = ☐

2) 6 x 12 = ☐   18) 7 x 12 = ☐   34) 3 x 12 = ☐

3) 10 x 12 = ☐   19) 2 x 12 = ☐   35) 12 x 12 = ☐

4) 5 x 12 = ☐   20) 6 x 12 = ☐   36) 11 x 12 = ☐

5) 12 x 12 = ☐   21) 2 x 12 = ☐   37) 1 x 12 = ☐

6) 4 x 12 = ☐   22) 9 x 12 = ☐   38) 5 x 12 = ☐

7) 7 x 12 = ☐   23) 4x 12 = ☐   39) 10 x 12 = ☐

8) 11 x 12 = ☐   24) 8 x 12 = ☐   40) 3 x 12 = ☐

9) ☐ x 12 = 24   25) ☐ x 12 = 60   41) ☐ x 12 = 72

10) ☐ x 12 = 72   26) ☐ x 12 = 36   42) ☐ x 12 = 12

11) ☐ x 12 = 132   27) ☐ x 12 = 108   43) ☐ x 12 = 36

12) ☐ x 12 = 144   28) ☐ x 12 = 12   44) ☐ x 12 = 84

13) ☐ x 12 = 108   29) ☐ x 12 = 48   45) ☐ x 12 = 96

14) ☐ x 12 = 84   30) ☐ x 12 = 120   46) ☐ x 12 = 132

15) ☐ x 12 = 60   31) ☐ x 12 = 144   47) ☐ x 12 = 24

16) ☐ x 12 = 120   32) ☐ x 12 = 48   48) ☐ x 12 = 96

The 11 and 12 Times Table Test

1) 12 x 12 = ☐   17)   5 x 12 = ☐   33)   4 x 12 = ☐

2)   8 x 11 = ☐   18) 12 x 11 = ☐   34)   5 x 11 = ☐

3) 10 x 12 = ☐   19)   1 x 12 = ☐   35)   7 x 12 = ☐

4) 11 x 11 = ☐   20)   7 x 11 = ☐   36)   4 x 11 = ☐

5)   8 x 12 = ☐   21)   9 x 12 = ☐   37)   2 x 12 = ☐

6)   6 x 11 = ☐   22) 10 x 11 = ☐   38)   9 x 11 = ☐

7) 11 x 12 = ☐   23)   3 x 12 = ☐   39)   6 x 12 = ☐

8)   3 x 11 = ☐   24)   2 x 11 = ☐   40)   1 x 11 = ☐

9) ☐ x 12 = 60   25) ☐ x 12 = 144   41) ☐ x 12 = 84

10) ☐ x 11 = 33   26) ☐ x 11 = 55   42) ☐ x 11 = 121

11) ☐ x 12 = 120   27) ☐ x 12 = 48   43) ☐ x 12 = 36

12) ☐ x 11 = 66   28) ☐ x 11 = 110   44) ☐ x 11 = 99

13) ☐ x 12 = 24   29) ☐ x 12 = 12   45) ☐ x 12 = 108

14) ☐ x 11 = 88   30) ☐ x 11 = 44   46) ☐ x 11 = 11

15) ☐ x 12 = 72   31) ☐ x 12 = 132   47) ☐ x 12 = 96

16) ☐ x 11 = 22   32) ☐ x 11 = 77   48) ☐ x 11 = 132

The 9, 10, 11 and 12 Times Table Test

1) 12 x 10 = ☐   17) 1 x 10 = ☐   33) 8 x 10 = ☐

2) 7 x 9 = ☐   18) 11 x 9 = ☐   34) 2 x 9 = ☐

3) 10 x 11 = ☐   19) 6 x 11 = ☐   35) 3 x 11 = ☐

4) 6 x 12 = ☐   20) 1 x 12 = ☐   36) 8 x 12 = ☐

5) 7 x 10 = ☐   21) 4 x 10 = ☐   37) 3 x 10 = ☐

6) 1 x 9 = ☐   22) 12 x 9 = ☐   38) 5 x 9 = ☐

7) 11 x 11 = ☐   23) 9 x 11 = ☐   39) 5 x 11 = ☐

8) 10 x 12 = ☐   24) 4 x 12 = ☐   40) 12 x 12 = ☐

9) ☐ x 10 = 50   25) ☐ x 10 = 110   41) ☐ x 10 = 90

10) ☐ x 9 = 36   26) ☐ x 9 = 54   42) ☐ x 9 = 27

11) ☐ x 11 = 44   27) ☐ x 11 = 88   43) ☐ x 11 = 22

12) ☐ x 12 = 36   28) ☐ x 12 = 108   44) ☐ x 12 = 84

13) ☐ x 10 = 60   29) ☐ x 10 = 20   45) ☐ x 10 = 100

14) ☐ x 9 = 81   30) ☐ x 9 = 72   46) ☐ x 9 = 90

15) ☐ x 11 = 11   31) ☐ x 11 = 132   47) ☐ x 11 = 77

16) ☐ x 12 = 60   32) ☐ x 12 = 144   48) ☐ x 12 = 24

The 7, 8, 9, 10, 11 and 12 Times Tables Test

1) 9 x 7 = ☐

2) 10 x 8 = ☐

3) 7 x 9 = ☐

4) 5 x 10 = ☐

5) 6 x 11 = ☐

6) 12 x 12 = ☐

7) 10 x 7 = ☐

8) 9 x 8 = ☐

9) ☐ x 9 = 108

10) ☐ x 10 = 70

11) ☐ x 11 = 88

12) ☐ x 12 = 72

13) ☐ x 7 = 84

14) ☐ x 8 = 56

15) ☐ x 9 = 72

16) ☐ x 10 = 120

17) 10 x 11 = ☐

18) 11 x 12 = ☐

19) 7 x 7 = ☐

20) 4 x 8 = ☐

21) 6 x 9 = ☐

22) 12 x 10 = ☐

23) 9 x 11 = ☐

24) 5 x 12 = ☐

25) ☐ x 7 = 35

26) ☐ x 8 = 48

27) ☐ x 9 = 81

28) ☐ x 10 = 100

29) ☐ x 11 = 121

30) ☐ x 12 = 84

31) ☐ x 7 = 42

32) ☐ x 8 = 88

33) 12 x 9 = ☐

34) 8 x 10 = ☐

35) 4 x 11 = ☐

36) 3 x 12 = ☐

37) 8 x 7 = ☐

38) 5 x 8 = ☐

39) 3 x 9 = ☐

40) 4 x 10 = ☐

41) ☐ x 11 = 132

42) ☐ x 12 = 48

43) ☐ x 7 = 28

44) ☐ x 8 = 64

45) ☐ x 9 = 99

46) ☐ x 10 = 90

47) ☐ x 11 = 77

48) ☐ x 12 = 24

The 1 to 12 Times Tables Test

1) 1 x 1 = ☐   17) 3 x 6 = ☐   33) 8 x 12 = ☐

2) 2 x 2 = ☐   18) 2 x 7 = ☐   34) 4 x 4 = ☐

3) 1 x 3 = ☐   19) 5 x 8 = ☐   35) 1 x 5 = ☐

4) 3 x 4 = ☐   20) 7 x 9 = ☐   36) 2 x 6 = ☐

5) 4 x 5 = ☐   21) 8 x 10 = ☐   37) 6 x 7 = ☐

6) 5 x 6 = ☐   22) 6 x 11 = ☐   38) 7 x 8 = ☐

7) 4 x 7 = ☐   23) 1 x 12 = ☐   39) 5 x 9 = ☐

8) 8 x 8 = ☐   24) 2 x 3 = ☐   40) 4 x 10 = ☐

9) ☐ x 9 = 81   25) ☐ x 4 = 4   41) ☐ x 11 = 22

10) ☐ x 10 = 60 26) ☐ x 5 = 25   42) ☐ x 12 = 36

11) ☐ x 11 = 110 27) ☐ x 6 = 24   43) ☐ x 5 = 10

12) ☐ x 12 = 84 28) ☐ x 7 = 35   44) ☐ x 6 = 36

13) ☐ x 2 = 2   29) ☐ x 8 = 24   45) ☐ x 7 = 7

14) ☐ x 3 = 9   30) ☐ x 9 = 18   46) ☐ x 8 = 32

15) ☐ x 4 = 8   31) ☐ x 10 = 10   47) ☐ x 9 = 9

16) ☐ x 5 = 15   32) ☐ x 11 = 44   48) ☐ x 10 = 30

The 1 to 12 Times Tables Test Continued

49) 9 x 11 = [   ]   59) 2 x 8 = [   ]   69) 3 x 9 = [   ]

50) 10 x 12 = [   ]   60) 4 x 9 = [   ]   70) 2 x 10 = [   ]

51) 1 x 6 = [   ]   61) 7 x 10 = [   ]   71) 7 x 11 = [   ]

52) 3 x 7 = [   ]   62) 11 x 11 = [   ]   72) 11 x 12 = [   ]

53) 6 x 8 = [   ]   63) 6 x 12 = [   ]   73) 9 x 10 = [   ]

54) [   ] x 9 = 54   64) [   ] x 8 = 8   74) [   ] x 11 = 11

55) [   ] x 10 = 100   65) [   ] x 9 = 72   75) [   ] x 12 = 24

56) [   ] x 11 = 88   66) [   ] x 10 = 50   76) [   ] x 11 = 55

57) [   ] x 12 = 48   67) [   ] x 11 = 33   77) [   ] x 12 = 144

58) [   ] x 7 = 49   68) [   ] x 12 = 108   78) [   ] x 12 = 60

Times Tables Tests Answers

1 Times Table

1) 3	17) 9	33) 10
2) 7	18) 10	34) 6
3) 8	19) 4	35) 12
4) 1	20) 1	36) 11
5) 8	21) 2	37) 4
6) 5	22) 5	38) 7
7) 11	23) 12	39) 9
8) 3	24) 6	40) 2
9) 4	25) 2	41) 12
10) 11	26) 10	42) 9
11) 5	27) 12	43) 2
12) 3	28) 6	44) 3
13) 9	29) 1	45) 6
14) 8	30) 7	46) 8
15) 1	31) 11	47) 10
16) 7	32) 4	48) 5

2 Times Table

1) 24	17) 12	33) 18
2) 14	18) 20	34) 10
3) 16	19) 8	35) 20
4) 2	20) 12	36) 24
5) 16	21) 4	37) 18
6) 10	22) 6	38) 22
7) 22	23) 14	39) 8
8) 2	24) 6	40) 4
9) 8	25) 10	41) 11
10) 6	26) 12	42) 5
11) 4	27) 9	43) 6
12) 11	28) 3	44) 4
13) 5	29) 8	45) 3
14) 2	30) 10	46) 9
15) 1	31) 7	47) 12
16) 7	32) 2	48) 1

1 & 2 Times Tables

1) 6	17) 22	33) 16
2) 5	18) 4	34) 7
3) 4	19) 14	35) 12
4) 6	20) 12	36) 2
5) 2	21) 10	37) 18
6) 8	22) 10	38) 9
7) 20	23) 24	39) 8
8) 3	24) 1	40) 11
9) 8	25) 5	41) 12
10) 4	26) 9	42) 11
11) 3	27) 9	43) 11
12) 10	28) 2	44) 5
13) 6	29) 10	45) 2
14) 12	30) 6	46) 7
15) 1	31) 14	47) 4
16) 1	32) 3	48) 8

3 Times Table

1) 9	17) 27	33) 6
2) 21	18) 30	34) 15
3) 36	19) 15	35) 36
4) 3	20) 18	36) 24
5) 24	21) 6	37) 27
6) 12	22) 18	38) 33
7) 3	23) 21	39) 12
8) 30	24) 9	40) 33
9) 2	25) 10	41) 11
10) 4	26) 8	42) 5
11) 3	27) 6	43) 2
12) 5	28) 11	44) 12
13) 12	29) 8	45) 3
14) 9	30) 9	46) 6
15) 7	31) 7	47) 10
16) 1	32) 3	48) 4

4 Times Table

1) 24	17) 44	33) 40
2) 28	18) 16	34) 20
3) 48	19) 8	35) 48
4) 40	20) 24	36) 32
5) 32	21) 8	37) 36
6) 36	22) 12	38) 4
7) 4	23) 28	39) 16
8) 20	24) 12	40) 44
9) 3	25) 1	41) 5
10) 5	26) 4	42) 3
11) 11	27) 2	43) 10
12) 7	28) 10	44) 9
13) 9	29) 1	45) 2
14) 8	30) 6	46) 4
15) 6	31) 12	47) 8
16) 12	32) 7	48) 11

3 & 4 Times Tables

1) 20	17) 4	33) 8
2) 21	18) 36	34) 9
3) 48	19) 36	35) 32
4) 6	20) 3	36) 3
5) 12	21) 28	37) 16
6) 15	22) 30	38) 18
7) 44	23) 40	39) 24
8) 27	24) 24	40) 33
9) 4	25) 8	41) 6
10) 11	26) 3	42) 5
11) 1	27) 5	43) 11
12) 6	28) 8	44) 12
13) 3	29) 7	45) 2
14) 1	30) 2	46) 9
15) 10	31) 12	47) 9
16) 10	32) 7	48) 4

1, 2, 3 & 4 Times Tables

1) 4	17) 12	33) 11
2) 12	18) 10	34) 4
3) 36	19) 6	35) 33
4) 40	20) 24	36) 4
5) 6	21) 1	37) 3
6) 16	22) 6	38) 8
7) 3	23) 21	39) 12
8) 20	24) 12	40) 44
9) 10	25) 7	41) 5
10) 7	26) 9	42) 11
11) 10	27) 3	43) 9
12) 7	28) 4	44) 9
13) 9	29) 2	45) 8
14) 1	30) 12	46) 10
15) 8	31) 6	47) 5
16) 12	32) 8	48) 2

5 Times Table

1) 45	17) 10	33) 50
2) 35	18) 20	34) 15
3) 60	19) 10	35) 60
4) 25	20) 30	36) 40
5) 40	21) 35	37) 45
6) 55	22) 15	38) 5
7) 50	23) 25	39) 20
8) 5	24) 30	40) 55
9) 6	25) 1	41) 4
10) 4	26) 3	42) 10
11) 5	27) 5	43) 5
12) 7	28) 11	44) 6
13) 10	29) 1	45) 11
14) 12	30) 12	46) 3
15) 9	31) 9	47) 7
16) 8	32) 2	48) 8

6 Times Table

1) 54	17) 36	33) 72
2) 24	18) 24	34) 18
3) 66	19) 12	35) 66
4) 30	20) 36	36) 6
5) 48	21) 42	37) 54
6) 60	22) 18	38) 30
7) 12	23) 60	39) 42
8) 6	24) 48	40) 72
9) 4	25) 2	41) 4
10) 10	26) 7	42) 10
11) 3	27) 12	43) 3
12) 6	28) 1	44) 5
13) 12	29) 11	45) 12
14) 5	30) 1	46) 6
15) 9	31) 7	47) 9
16) 8	32) 2	48) 8

5 & 6 Times Tables

1) 18	17) 30	33) 12
2) 45	18) 50	34) 25
3) 60	19) 48	35) 6
4) 30	20) 20	36) 40
5) 42	21) 54	37) 36
6) 10	22) 55	38) 35
7) 72	23) 66	39) 24
8) 60	24) 5	40) 15
9) 2	25) 5	41) 4
10) 11	26) 2	42) 10
11) 1	27) 3	43) 9
12) 1	28) 5	44) 12
13) 11	29) 12	45) 8
14) 6	30) 9	46) 3
15) 10	31) 7	47) 6
16) 8	32) 4	48) 7

1, 2, 3, 4, 5 & 6 Times Table

1) 48	17) 18	33) 16
2) 35	18) 11	34) 21
3) 44	19) 54	35) 14
4) 18	20) 40	36) 8
5) 16	21) 36	37) 24
6) 9	22) 36	38) 25
7) 60	23) 20	39) 32
8) 60	24) 5	40) 30
9) 5	25) 7	41) 11
10) 3	26) 11	42) 10
11) 5	27) 7	43) 8
12) 7	28) 9	44) 11
13) 12	29) 6	45) 6
14) 6	30) 12	46) 11
15) 2	31) 6	47) 12
16) 5	32) 4	48) 5

7 Times Table

1) 28	17) 42	33) 70
2) 21	18) 28	34) 63
3) 84	19) 14	35) 77
4) 35	20) 42	36) 84
5) 49	21) 63	37) 56
6) 70	22) 21	38) 35
7) 14	23) 77	39) 49
8) 7	24) 56	40) 7
9) 7	25) 3	41) 4
10) 12	26) 1	42) 1
11) 6	27) 4	43) 11
12) 10	28) 11	44) 9
13) 5	29) 8	45) 2
14) 2	30) 7	46) 5
15) 8	31) 6	47) 12
16) 9	32) 3	48) 10

8 Times Tables

#		#		#	
1)	32	17)	64	33)	80
2)	72	18)	32	34)	16
3)	96	19)	16	35)	80
4)	40	20)	48	36)	96
5)	56	21)	24	37)	88
6)	8	22)	72	38)	40
7)	48	23)	24	39)	56
8)	88	24)	64	40)	8
9)	3	25)	11	41)	4
10)	10	26)	6	42)	7
11)	7	27)	5	43)	3
12)	12	28)	9	44)	11
13)	2	29)	1	45)	2
14)	1	30)	6	46)	5
15)	4	31)	12	47)	8
16)	8	32)	10	48)	9

7 & 8 Times Table

#		#		#	
1)	64	17)	24	33)	32
2)	28	18)	84	34)	56
3)	80	19)	16	35)	8
4)	63	20)	42	36)	21
5)	40	21)	56	37)	72
6)	7	22)	70	38)	35
7)	96	23)	88	39)	48
8)	77	24)	14	40)	49
9)	1	25)	4	41)	3
10)	5	26)	3	42)	6
11)	2	27)	10	43)	6
12)	2	28)	4	44)	9
13)	8	29)	9	45)	11
14)	12	30)	8	46)	1
15)	7	31)	5	47)	12
16)	11	32)	10	48)	7

5, 6, 7 & 8 Times Table

#		#		#	
1)	15	17)	50	33)	30
2)	54	18)	48	34)	42
3)	77	19)	14	35)	63
4)	80	20)	64	36)	8
5)	45	21)	55	37)	25
6)	12	22)	18	38)	66
7)	7	23)	49	39)	70
8)	40	24)	16	40)	88
9)	1	25)	7	41)	8
10)	4	26)	6	42)	12
11)	5	27)	8	43)	12
12)	3	28)	7	44)	9
13)	2	29)	4	45)	12
14)	1	30)	10	46)	5
15)	4	31)	7	47)	6
16)	6	32)	4	48)	12

9 Times Table

#		#		#	
1)	9	17)	72	33)	99
2)	54	18)	36	34)	27
3)	90	19)	18	35)	108
4)	45	20)	63	36)	99
5)	81	21)	18	37)	90
6)	36	22)	81	38)	45
7)	54	23)	27	39)	63
8)	108	24)	72	40)	9
9)	2	25)	8	41)	4
10)	5	26)	4	42)	6
11)	6	27)	10	43)	3
12)	12	28)	9	44)	10
13)	11	29)	5	45)	2
14)	1	30)	1	46)	11
15)	3	31)	12	47)	7
16)	7	32)	9	48)	8

10 Times Table

#		#		#	
1)	120	17)	10	33)	20
2)	70	18)	110	34)	70
3)	100	19)	40	35)	30
4)	20	20)	50	36)	90
5)	80	21)	60	37)	80
6)	40	22)	110	38)	10
7)	120	23)	90	39)	50
8)	100	24)	30	40)	60
9)	5	25)	12	41)	5
10)	4	26)	6	42)	3
11)	1	27)	3	43)	8
12)	2	28)	11	44)	9
13)	6	29)	7	45)	10
14)	9	30)	4	46)	2
15)	7	31)	11	47)	10
16)	8	32)	1	48)	12

9 & 10 Times Tables

#		#		#	
1)	120	17)	10	33)	20
2)	63	18)	99	34)	72
3)	100	19)	40	35)	30
4)	45	20)	18	36)	81
5)	70	21)	60	37)	80
6)	9	22)	108	38)	36
7)	110	23)	90	39)	50
8)	90	24)	27	40)	54
9)	5	25)	12	41)	4
10)	4	26)	6	42)	3
11)	1	27)	8	43)	3
12)	2	28)	12	44)	9
13)	6	29)	7	45)	10
14)	9	30)	5	46)	7
15)	2	31)	11	47)	9
16)	8	32)	1	48)	11

11 Times Table

#		#		#	
1)	99	17)	22	33)	11
2)	66	18)	44	34)	55
3)	110	19)	33	35)	132
4)	88	20)	77	36)	121
5)	110	21)	88	37)	55
6)	44	22)	99	38)	11
7)	77	23)	33	39)	121
8)	132	24)	66	40)	22
9)	3	25)	8	41)	4
10)	6	26)	9	42)	7
11)	11	27)	12	43)	2
12)	10	28)	5	44)	1
13)	11	29)	4	45)	8
14)	7	30)	10	46)	3
15)	5	31)	9	47)	1
16)	12	32)	2	48)	6

12 Times Table

#		#		#	
1)	108	17)	96	33)	12
2)	72	18)	84	34)	36
3)	120	19)	24	35)	144
4)	60	20)	72	36)	132
5)	144	21)	24	37)	12
6)	48	22)	108	38)	60
7)	84	23)	48	39)	120
8)	132	24)	96	40)	36
9)	2	25)	5	41)	6
10)	6	26)	3	42)	1
11)	11	27)	9	43)	3
12)	12	28)	1	44)	7
13)	9	29)	4	45)	8
14)	7	30)	10	46)	11
15)	5	31)	12	47)	2
16)	10	32)	4	48)	8

11 & 12 Times Tables

#		#		#	
1)	144	17)	60	33)	48
2)	88	18)	132	34)	55
3)	120	19)	12	35)	84
4)	121	20)	77	36)	44
5)	96	21)	108	37)	24
6)	66	22)	110	38)	99
7)	132	23)	36	39)	72
8)	32	24)	22	40)	11
9)	5	25)	12	41)	7
10)	3	26)	5	42)	11
11)	10	27)	4	43)	3
12)	6	28)	10	44)	9
13)	2	29)	1	45)	9
14)	8	30)	4	46)	1
15)	6	31)	11	47)	8
16)	2	32)	7	48)	12

9, 10, 11 & 12 Times Tables

#		#		#	
1)	120	17)	10	33)	80
2)	63	18)	99	34)	18
3)	110	19)	66	35)	33
4)	72	20)	12	36)	96
5)	70	21)	40	37)	30
6)	9	22)	108	38)	45
7)	121	23)	99	39)	55
8)	120	24)	48	40)	144
9)	5	25)	11	41)	9
10)	4	26)	6	42)	3
11)	4	27)	8	43)	2
12)	3	28)	9	44)	7
13)	6	29)	2	45)	10
14)	9	30)	8	46)	10
15)	1	31)	12	47)	7
16)	5	32)	12	48)	2

7, 8, 9, 10, 11 & 12 Times Tables

#		#		#	
1)	63	17)	110	33)	108
2)	80	18)	132	34)	80
3)	63	19)	49	35)	44
4)	50	20)	32	36)	36
5)	66	21)	54	37)	56
6)	144	22)	120	38)	40
7)	70	23)	99	39)	27
8)	72	24)	60	40)	40
9)	12	25)	5	41)	12
10)	7	26)	6	42)	4
11)	8	27)	9	43)	4
12)	6	28)	10	44)	8
13)	12	29)	11	45)	11
14)	7	30)	7	46)	9
15)	8	31)	6	47)	7
16)	12	32)	11	48)	2

1 to 12 Times Tables

#		#		#	
1)	1	17)	18	33)	96
2)	4	18)	14	34)	16
3)	3	19)	40	35)	5
4)	12	20)	63	36)	12
5)	20	21)	80	37)	42
6)	30	22)	66	38)	56
7)	28	23)	12	39)	45
8)	64	24)	6	40)	40
9)	9	25)	1	41)	2
10)	6	26)	5	42)	3
11)	10	27)	4	43)	2
12)	7	28)	5	44)	6
13)	1	29)	3	45)	1
14)	3	30)	2	46)	4
15)	2	31)	1	47)	1
16)	3	32)	4	48)	3

1 to 12 Times Tables Continued

49) 99	59) 16	69) 27
50) 120	60) 36	70) 20
51) 6	61) 70	71) 77
52) 21	62) 121	72) 132
53) 48	63) 72	73) 90
54) 6	64) 1	74) 1
55) 10	65) 8	75) 2
56) 8	66) 5	76) 5
57) 4	67) 3	77) 12
58) 7	68) 9	78) 5

Please leave a review on Amazon

If you have enjoyed this book, I would very much appreciate it if you left me a review on the Amazon website. Just search for "Mastering Multiplication Tables".
Thank you very much,
C P James

Printed in Great Britain
by Amazon.co.uk, Ltd.,
Marston Gate.